Dear Lauren,

THE NEW FAMILY TABLE

COOKING MORE, EATING TOGETHER & STAYING (RELATIVELY) SANE

chef JULIA NORDGREN, MD

I hope you enjoy the book!

♡ Julia

THE NEW FAMILY TABLE

COOKING MORE, EATING TOGETHER & STAYING (RELATIVELY) SANE

chef JULIA NORDGREN, MD

photography by Jennifer Davick

STORY FARM

WINTER PARK • MIAMI • SANTA BARBARA

The New Family Table: Cooking More, Eating Together & Staying (Relatively) Sane
Copyright ©2019 by Julia Nordgren, MD
Photography copyright ©2019 by Jennifer Davick

All rights reserved. No part of this book may be reproduced in any manner without the express written permission of Julia Nordgren, M.D., and Story Farm, Inc., except in the context of reviews.

Published in the United States of America by Story Farm, Inc.
www.story-farm.com

Library of Congress-Cataloging-in-Publication Data available upon request.

ISBN 978-1-7326456-0-8

EDITORIAL DIRECTOR Joan Tapper
CREATIVE DIRECTOR Lauren Eggert
COPY EDITORS Karen Cakebread, Billie Jo Spencer, Ashley Fraxedas
INDEXING Amy Hall
PRODUCTION MANAGEMENT Tina Dahl

Printed in China

10 9 8 7 6 5 4 3 2 1
First Edition January 2019

Additonal Photography by:
Kristina Todini—27, 40, 46, 53, 57, 59, 72, 82, 99, 126, 147, 155
Kerry Shutz—14, 23, 24, 64, 73, 77, 83, 102, 105
Mark Leet—6, 8, 49, 60, 90, 112, 142

FOR MY FAMILY

AND YOURS

TABLE OF CONTENTS

INTRODUCTION — 9

BREAKFAST: *better beginnings* — 12

SNACKS: *bridging the gap* — 38

VEGETABLES: *from concept to reality* — 62

SOUPS, STEWS & MAKEAHEADS: *strategies for sanity* — 88

DINNER: *mainly delicious* — 110

DESSERTS: *the art of the flip* — 140

ACKNOWLEDGMENTS — 166

INTRODUCTION

I have always been wild about being a pediatrician. While my job is less glamorous than *Grey's Anatomy* might suggest, caring for children is a fun and dynamic way to be a doctor. I love so much about it—taking care of sweet, sleepy newborns, watching toddlers bumble around the office, chatting with talkative kindergarteners, even helping sassy teens navigate their complex world and unique health risks. I have always loved working with parents, helping them become more knowledgeable and confident in their ever-changing job of raising healthy and happy people. I love our sense of common purpose. At my core, I just really love kids. Despite the many exhausting aggravations of the job, being a pediatrician has always felt like fun for me.

But seven years into my general practice, I started to feel worn down by a persistent, overwhelming problem that I was ill-equipped to solve: the childhood obesity epidemic was taking firm hold and eroding the health of so many of my patients. Excess weight seemed to make everything worse, from asthma to knee pain to struggles in school and with friends. And so many of these issues were rooted in everyday eating habits.

Like many pediatricians, I felt limited in my ability to counsel around food. I could give chipper endorsements to eat more vegetables and fruits. Avoid soda. Read food labels. I had some fun handouts. But I didn't have much time to dedicate to nutrition, and my well-intentioned advice wasn't translating into healthier habits.

I realized that to be a truly effective pediatrician, I needed to know how to really help people eat well—every day, over time—to shift to better core eating habits. Not just at home but at school and in restaurants. Not just with a catchphrase or a colorful handout but with real, specific, impactful advice that a family could actually use. And enjoy. I needed to know a lot more about food. I wanted to know how to cook—I mean *really* cook—and teach my patients to do the same.

I thought a lot about how I could go about doing this. I looked into dozens of nutrition and cooking programs. After a couple of years of dreaming, thinking, talking, and planning, I took a big plunge. I took a break from my medical practice to become a chef. I traded my stethoscope for a set of knives and enrolled at the Culinary Institute of America in California.

Pursuing culinary training was an incredible experience. It was very hard work. I learned skills, techniques, and recipes. I learned the language of food, about different food cultures, about ingredients and techniques from all over the world. Being a doctor in the kitchen had an upside: I could treat minor burns! I could treat minor knife wounds! Occasionally I was teased for my health consciousness, but I knew that my two loves, food and medicine, had more in common than people realized.

My pursuit of culinary training was not at all to abandon my practice of medicine, but to enhance it. And now that I am back in the office, my understanding about food is at the core of how I care for patients. I specialize in children with cholesterol disorders or prediabetes and kids who are overweight or obese. So to all of my patients, food matters a lot. And I can really help parents do one of the most essential things to help their children be healthy: cook.

Now, I know not everyone loves to cook. Planning and preparing meals makes a lot of people edgy and anxious. It can feel overwhelming with so much else going on. Between work schedules, sports, and activities, cooking can move off the priority list. It isn't hard to outsource dinner. There are times when convenience is more important than anything else. But as a doctor who sees the major downside of eating out, I want to share two important things I have learned.

First, cooking matters. It is the best defense we have in a world where we are inundated with quick, convenient, nutrient-poor, oversized foods that are compromising our health. The foods we buy in restaurants are far heavier in salt, fat, sugar, and calories than what we would make at home. Cooking gives us invaluable control over the quality of ingredients and how a dish is prepared. As parents, we care far more about the healthfulness of a meal than any profit-driven restaurant or food company does. With rare exceptions, any meal cooked at home is healthier than a meal eaten out.

Second, connecting matters. It is important to gather with the people who are important to us. Eating together as a family is one of the most important opportunities we have to enhance the physical, intellectual, and emotional growth of our children. Countless studies show how family dinners have a positive impact: children who eat regularly with their families consume more fruits and vegetables, are less likely to be obese, have stronger language development, and are even at less risk of substance abuse. Eating together is one of the few things we can do that helps *everything*.

It thrills me to see that family dinners are back on the rise. I see so many signs of a renewed commitment to cooking at home and eating together. More and more, families are reclaiming that space, protecting dinnertime, and putting aside devices for the important ritual of family dinner conversation. I love hearing people talk about how much they are enjoying more time together at the table, both kids and parents. And while it isn't always fun, having a media-free dinner always matters.

Also on the rise is the demand for healthy, fresh, nutritious whole foods. I love seeing lively crowds at farmers markets. I love seeing talented chefs shine a light on quality, locally sourced ingredients. It is great to see companies thrive by providing organic, plant-forward meal kits to busy families. I even love seeing my Instagram feed full of colorful vegetable stands and delicious breakfast bowls. I love how we all inspire each other to try something new and to cook even better.

This, to me, is what *The New Family Table* is all about. It is about feeling truly motivated by wanting to do right by the people we love. It is about knowing that this is our time to nourish our children or whoever is around us. It is about reclaiming our purpose to eat together, to know each other, and to enjoy each other. It is about shifting toward better ingredients, healthier foods, and more vibrant flavors one simple meal at a time.

In the recipes that follow, you will find the building blocks of great eating. You won't find anything difficult, fussy, or overly expensive. You will see basic cooking techniques that you can adapt to your fami-

ly's preferences and the ingredients around you. You will see a little bit of everything, which is a reflection of not only my personal style but also a pattern of eating that I see works for many successful families. I focus on eating a lot of vegetables, plant-based proteins, whole grains, nuts, and legumes. I include dairy and meat, but you certainly are welcome to make your own choices. There are many ways to eat healthfully, and I want you to find a way that works well and that you enjoy.

These recipes are also designed to reflect what is new about the family table—the influence of global cuisine all around us. Indian flavors, Mexican spices, Asian cooking techniques, and Mediterranean eating are all a part of our rich food landscape, and it is easier than you might think to bring that to your own family table.

Being a trained chef has made being a pediatrician even more fun and dynamic. It helps me far beyond my colorful handouts and well-intentioned nutrition advice. I can connect with families through my knowledge as a doctor, my true love of food, and my struggles as a working parent. My job still isn't easy and glamorous, but there is nothing more rewarding than helping a child eat better, feel healthier, enjoy food and have more time at the table with his or her family.

I do hope this book helps you, wherever you are in your journey in the kitchen. Just like I tell my own kids, I want to help you cook for the people you love and talk to them while you eat.

Enjoy!

BREAKFAST
BETTER BEGINNINGS

I am often asked to weigh in on the age-old question of the morning meal: Is it true? Is breakfast really the most important meal of the day?

Yes! I say.

And no. At least, not in the way you might think.

The first meal of the day matters a lot. What we start our day with—the quality of food, the ingredients, and the balance of nutrients—sets our metabolic stage for the rest of the day.

What matters a lot less is the timing of the meal. It doesn't matter to me what time that first meal is. Whether "breakfast" happens at 7 a.m. or 9 a.m. or noon is not critical. It is what is eaten first that makes it so important.

The first meal and, specifically, how the first meal affects your blood sugar, sets the tone for the rest of the day. A breakfast high in sugar or simple carbohydrates—think cereal, a plain bagel, or a granola bar—will send your blood sugar rising. This holds hunger at bay for the moment, but it comes with a blood sugar drop 90 minutes later. This leads us to feel hungry, cranky, and unable to concentrate. Our brain sends us searching for more carbohydrates, and the blood-sugar roller coaster continues.

That is why the "something is better than nothing" philosophy backfires when applied to breakfast. Most convenient breakfast foods actually promote weight gain and blood sugar instability. These highly processed carbohydrate choices (almost everything in the cereal aisle!) often do far more harm than good.

What we all need in the morning are the tried-and-true essentials. We need healthy protein, fiber, and even healthy fats. We need the vitamins, minerals, and phytochemicals of fruits, vegetables, and whole grains. These are the building blocks of good energy, stable blood sugars, and overall good health.

This breakfast chapter focuses on dishes that can be worked into a hectic morning or prepped the night before. They are all based on nourishing ingredients and won't send you on a metabolic roller coaster. And, of course, these recipes are all delicious.

So enjoy a breakfast that works better for your body. And enjoy letting your cranky teenager sleep a little later!

GREEK YOGURT WITH CHERRIES & SLIVERED ALMONDS
SERVES 1

Have you ever found yourself staring blankly at the dairy case, confused by the dizzying array of yogurt choices? Me too.

I have solved this dilemma by realizing a simple truth. Most commercially flavored yogurt has a lot of sugar or is made with sugar alternatives, additives, and a long list of ingredients I can't even pronounce. It is much simpler—and infinitely healthier—to stick with plain yogurt and flavor it yourself. While plain yogurt can be a little too tangy for most kids, you can easily make it delicious with a zip of maple syrup, honey, or sugar.

My favorite combination includes cherries and slivered almonds, but use whatever fruit and nut you like.

1. Combine yogurt and sweetener in a small bowl. Taste and adjust to preferred sweetness. (You might find you need less sugar over time.)

2. Top with cherries and slivered almonds.

1 cup plain Greek yogurt

½ to 1 teaspoon natural sweetener (sugar, brown sugar, maple syrup, or honey)

8 to 10 fresh cherries, pits removed, sliced

1 to 2 tablespoons slivered almonds

HERE'S ANOTHER FRUIT-NUT OPTION

Cut a Granny Smith apple into small dice, and mix with 1 teaspoon each of cinnamon and sugar. Top each serving of yogurt with 2 tablespoons apple-cinnamon mixture and 1 tablespoon each of walnuts and raisins. If you have extra apple-cinnamon mixture, you can stir it into some steel-cut oats or regular oatmeal.

STEEL-CUT OATS WITH PEACHES

SERVES 4

I confess, I have never been a fan of traditional oatmeal. Steel-cut oats were an incredible discovery for me when they were served at a Healthy Kitchens, Healthy Lives conference. Finally, a hot cereal I could love!

Steel-cut oats have a fantastic texture; they are nutty and hold up well to fruit and nut toppings. With just a touch of sweetener and fruit, they give you an ideal start to the day. The secret to their nutritious properties lies in the way they're cut. You get more fiber and protein than in a more processed, flatter oat. The flip side is that these take some time to cook. One solution is to make them ahead; I often cook them while we are doing dinner dishes.

3 cups water

1 cup steel-cut oats (such as Bob's Red Mill®)

½ teaspoon kosher salt

1 teaspoon vanilla extract

2 peaches, sliced or cubed

¼ cup pure maple syrup

1. Bring water to a boil in a heavy-bottomed saucepan. Stir in oats, salt, and vanilla. Reduce heat to a low simmer and cook, stirring occasionally, 20 to 25 minutes.

2. Spoon into bowls and top each serving with a quarter of the peaches and 1 to 2 teaspoons maple syrup. Serve right away.

3. To serve later, pack oatmeal into individual storage containers and refrigerate. Reheat as needed and add peaches and maple syrup just before eating.

GOOD NEWS IF YOU ARE SHORT ON TIME: THERE IS AN EASY OVERNIGHT TECHNIQUE!

Place water in a heavy-bottomed saucepan. Bring to a boil and stir in oats, salt, and vanilla. • Cover and turn the heat off. Leave the oats on the burner and allow to sit overnight. • In the morning, stir well and reheat on the stovetop or in the microwave, adding more liquid if necessary. • Top with fruit and sweetener of your choice.

PERFECT EGGS
SERVES 2

OK, I know it sounds simple. But there is some skill involved in making a perfect hard-boiled egg. Mastering the process ensures that you can always prepare a delicious, satisfying, protein-rich breakfast or snack for yourself. I take hard-boiled eggs along when I have to leave the house early and know I will need something to eat in an hour or two

1. Place eggs in a pot of cold water. Heat the water until it just starts to boil.

2. Turn off the heat but leave the pot on the burner. Cover the pot, and let the eggs sit in the hot water for 8 to 12 minutes, depending on how you like your yolk. Be sure to set a timer!

- 8 minutes: soft boiled—the yolk is a little runny
- 10 minutes: medium— the yolk is still tender in the middle
- 12 minutes: hard boiled—the yolk is cooked throughout

4 eggs

Kosher salt

Freshly ground pepper, to taste

Olive oil, fresh herbs (optional)

3. When the timer goes off, pour off the hot water and cover eggs with cold water. Allow eggs to sit in the cold water a few minutes so they are cool enough to handle.

4. Roll each egg on all sides to break up the shell. Under cold running water, peel the egg by getting under the layer of skin so it separates easily.

5. If you are eating the egg at home, slice it in half, drizzle with olive oil, sprinkle with salt and pepper, and garnish with fresh herbs. Thyme and marjoram are my favorites.

Otherwise, place the egg in a to-go container and eat when you are ready.

OUR FAVORITE GRANOLA

SERVES 8

The biggest endorsement for this recipe came from my dear friend Sue. I had updated this recipe on my website to give it a different flavor profile. She emailed me immediately, clamoring for this version. It turns out she makes my granola every Sunday and brings it to work every day with Greek yogurt. Given that Sue is a busy doctor and has three kids, she can't mess around with a lousy breakfast. I just love that this recipe helps keep her on the go.

1. Preheat oven to 325°F.

2. Line 2 large baking sheets with parchment paper.

3. In a large bowl, mix together oats, almonds, pecans, walnuts, cinnamon, allspice, salt, vanilla, and maple syrup. Taste and add more seasonings as you see fit. The mixture

3 cups thick rolled oats

1 cup chopped almonds

1 cup chopped pecans

1 cup chopped walnuts

1½ tablespoons cinnamon, or more to taste

2 teaspoons allspice

1 teaspoon kosher salt

2 teaspoons vanilla extract

⅓ cup pure maple syrup, or more to taste

2 large egg whites

»

BETTER BREAKFAST | 23

should be flavorful and moist. If it still seems dry, add more maple syrup.

4. Lightly whisk egg whites and combine with the oat-nut mixture.

5. Spread granola on the baking sheets and bake until it is evenly toasted, 30 to 35 minutes. Halfway through cooking, rotate the baking sheets and stir granola so it all browns evenly.

6. Let cool. The granola keeps well in an airtight container for up to 2 weeks.

KEY TECHNIQUE
TASTE & ADJUST

One of the most important techniques to develop is tasting and adjusting. For this granola, if it doesn't taste flavorful when raw, it won't taste good cooked. It is so important to try it, think a minute, and add more seasonings if needed. You might need more cinnamon. You might need a little more salt. You might want to try adding some ground ginger. The most important thing is to taste everything and practice adjusting until it tastes good to you.

Be brave and make the recipe your own!

ALL ABOUT MILK

As a pediatrician, I am asked all the time about milk. How much is enough? How much is too much? What percentage of fat should I buy? Can I substitute plant-based milks and still get proper nutrition?

These are all great questions. Milk is always front and center in the national dialogue about dietary habits, especially for children. Calcium and vitamin D are key nutrients for bone health, and milk is a good source of both. There are many other sources of these important nutrients, however, including some great options for those who don't eat or drink dairy products. Getting calcium and vitamin D from other sources like broccoli, green leafy vegetables, tofu, and fish is a wise way to go too.

Since the variety of milk (or lack of milk) in a regular diet can have important health implications, you should talk to your doctor about what's right for you and your family.

Here are some general guidelines:

For most children, 16 to 24 ounces (2 to 3 cups) of milk a day is plenty. For some children, too much milk can be an appetite suppressant and interfere with eating nutrients found in other foods.

FLAVORED MILKS, like chocolate, vanilla, or strawberry, tend to be very high in added sugar. It is usually best to avoid them. This is also true for flavored almond milk or soy milk.

If your family drinks **COW'S MILK,** low-fat and nonfat dairy products are typically recommended for day-to-day consumption. On occasion, full-fat dairy products, like whole-milk yogurt, should also be fine, as is using whole milk in a recipe. Lactose-free milk is widely available for those who have trouble digesting lactose.

If you choose not to use dairy products, there are several options. Many plant-based milk products are now widely available. You'll see milk made out of soy, almonds, cashews, oats, rice, and even hemp seeds. Many of these products are fortified with vitamin D and calcium.

SOY MILK is made by steeping ground soybeans in water. It is the closest to dairy milk in terms of protein and fat content, and it tends to work well in recipes as a substitute for milk, particularly in baking. Some soy milks have a neutral flavor, while some have a soy aftertaste. It may be worth trying different brands to see which you like best.

NUT MILKS are typically made by soaking ground nuts and straining out the pulp. This leaves some nut flavor, but without the pulp, there isn't much left in terms of fiber or protein content. This is why nut milks can be lower in protein and calories than dairy or soy milks. They don't tend to perform the same way in recipes as dairy milks do, and they might need a thickener to achieve comparable results. Many people enjoy nut milks with cereal, over steel-cut oats, in smoothies, or just to drink.

RICE, OAT, AND HEMP MILKS tend to be the highest in carbohydrate content and the lowest in protein or fat. Like nut milks, they also don't work quite the same in recipes as a dairy milk or soy milk. Looking for a fortified option helps to ensure you are getting good nutrients.

COCONUT MILK *typically comes in cans in a full-fat version or a light version. It has the most saturated fat of plant-based milks. Its creaminess and flavor are what make it work for things like Thai soups or Indian stews. There are also coconut milk products packaged for drinking. These are made by adding water (and sometimes stabilizers) to pressed coconut milk.*

There might not be one right milk or milk alternative for you or your family. Make sure you are reading labels and evaluating the nutrient profile, particularly for calcium and vitamin D. And with so many products on the market, feel free to experiment!

BERRY-BANANA SMOOTHIE WITH ALMOND MILK

SERVES 2

This recipe is one way to encourage kids to be more self-sufficient in the kitchen. With these ingredients on hand, they can easily whip up a healthy smoothie.

We almost always have berries in the house. When I see them starting to become overripe, I pop them into small plastic freezer bags. I do the same with bananas; I peel them first and put them in individual bags. Both will keep in the freezer for 2 to 3 months.

1 cup fresh or frozen strawberries

1 banana, fresh or frozen

1½ cups unsweetened almond milk or milk of your choice

6 ice cubes (only if using all fresh fruit)

1. Place strawberries, banana, almond milk, and ice cubes in a blender. Omit ice cubes if the fruit is frozen. Puree until smooth.

2. Pour into 2 glasses and serve immediately.

ALMOND & BLUEBERRY WAFFLES

SERVES 4

These healthy, delicious waffles are a great alternative to packaged frozen waffles. They are amazing fresh or can be made in advance, wrapped well, and frozen. On busy mornings you can just toast and go!

1. Preheat waffle iron.

2. Sift together flours, baking powder, salt, and cinnamon. Set aside.

3. Whisk together buttermilk, eggs, melted butter, and vanilla. Slowly stir in the dry ingredients until just blended. The mixture may be lumpy, which is fine.

4. Ladle the batter into the hot waffle iron and sprinkle with blueberries. Cook until browned on both sides.

NOTE: An easy substitute for buttermilk is to measure a scant 1½ cups of low-fat milk and stir in 1½ tablespoons of lemon juice. Let sit 30 minutes and proceed with recipe.

¾ cup oat flour

¾ cup almond flour

1 cup all-purpose flour

2 teaspoons baking powder

¼ teaspoon salt

1 teaspoon cinnamon

1½ cups buttermilk (see note)

2 eggs

5 tablespoons melted butter, cooled

1 teaspoon vanilla extract

1 pint fresh blueberries

APPLE CINNAMON MUFFINS

MAKES 12 MUFFINS

Muffins are an adorable, transportable breakfast or snack that we all love. But most muffins sold would fit more into the category of dessert; they are usually loaded with butter and sugar. The ones you find at supermarkets or coffee shops are really just cupcakes without frosting.

These muffins are a better way to start the day. They are full of great, healthy ingredients—apples, whole-grain flour, almond flour, and avocado oil. Cinnamon and allspice bring them to life. This is a hearty, delicious breakfast (and, yes, it makes a good snack or dessert, too).

1. Preheat oven to 350°F.

2. Line muffin tins with parchment or foil liners.

3. Whisk together eggs, oil, applesauce, vanilla, brown sugar, and shredded apples in a large mixing bowl. Set aside.

4. In a medium bowl, whisk together flour, almond meal, baking powder, baking soda, cinnamon, allspice, cloves, and salt.

5. Gradually stir the dry ingredients into the wet ingredients until blended. Do not overmix.

6. Divide batter evenly among muffin cups. Bake until a toothpick inserted in the middle comes out clean, 22 to 25 minutes.

NOTE: You can shred the apples with a box grater, but it saves time to use a food processor with a shredding blade. No need to peel the apples.

2 eggs

½ cup avocado oil

½ cup unsweetened applesauce

2 teaspoons vanilla extract

½ cup brown sugar

2 heaping cups shredded apples (a combination of red and green works best; see note)

1¾ cups whole-wheat pastry flour

½ cup almond meal

1 teaspoon baking powder

½ teaspoon baking soda

1 tablespoon cinnamon

1 teaspoon allspice

1 teaspoon ground cloves

½ teaspoon kosher salt

PANCAKE PERFECTION

SERVES 4-6

I love pancakes just as much as the next girl. But I don't love the food coma I get afterward. So I didn't make them often until I came up with this recipe, dubbed by my family as Pancake Perfection.

These pancakes cover all the bases. Their fresh, nutritious ingredients combine to create a light yet hearty pancake. With some ripe berries and a steamy cup of coffee, this is a perfect breakfast!

1. Preheat oven to 250°F. Line a baking sheet with parchment paper.

2. Mix together flour, oat bran, baking powder, baking soda, and salt in a large bowl. Set aside.

3. In a separate bowl, whisk together eggs, brown sugar, almond milk, yogurt, vanilla, and avocado oil.

4. Working in batches, fold the dry ingredients into the wet ingredients. Stir gently until combined, taking care not to overmix the batter, or your pancakes will be tough.

5. Heat a large pan or griddle over medium heat. Once it's hot, lightly brush with butter or oil. Working in batches, pour ¼ cup batter per pancake into the pan and cook until bubbles arise on the surface and the bottom is golden brown, 1 to 2 minutes. Flip with a spatula and cook other side. Lightly oil pan in between batches, if needed.

6. Transfer pancakes to prepared baking sheet and place in preheated oven to keep warm until all pancakes are cooked and ready to serve.

7. Serve with pure maple syrup and an overflowing handful of berries.

1¾ cups whole-wheat pastry flour

¼ cup oat bran

2 teaspoons baking powder

1 teaspoon baking soda

½ teaspoon salt

2 eggs

2 tablespoons brown sugar

1 cup almond milk

1 cup plain whole-milk yogurt

2 teaspoons vanilla extract

3 tablespoons avocado oil

2 tablespoons butter or oil for pan

Pure maple syrup for serving

1 pint raspberries or blueberries for serving

SWEET POTATO BURRITOS

SERVES 4-6

This recipe was inspired by my friend's amazing daughter, Eleanor. I have watched her grow from a smart, soulful half-pint to a brilliant, curious, and absolutely lovely young woman. She and her family love to eat, and this is one of Eleanor's favorite meals. If this powers her days, it can power mine—and yours!

1. Preheat oven to 375°F.

2. Scrub sweet potatoes and pierce in several places with a fork. Place on a baking sheet and set in the middle rack of the oven. Bake until soft, about 40 minutes. Let cool. (See note.)

3. Turn oven down to 250°F. Wrap tortillas in foil and place in oven until ready to use.

4. Heat a sauté pan over medium-high heat, then add oil. Add onion and cook until soft, about 5 minutes. Add garlic and cook 1 more minute, until garlic is fragrant. Add salt, pepper, paprika, and chili powder, and continue to cook, 1 to 2 minutes.

5. Add black beans and water, and cook over medium heat until beans are warm and water has evaporated, 5 to 7 minutes. Remove from heat.

6. Remove sweet potato skins and discard. Mash sweet potatoes with a fork and add a couple generous pinches of salt and pepper.

7. Lay out warm tortillas. Divide sweet potato mixture equally onto the tortillas. Add bean mixture and salsa.

8. Top with Greek yogurt, cilantro, and/or shredded cheese. Fold up the bottom edge of the burrito, then roll it lengthwise. Serve immediately or wrap in foil and take it to go!

NOTE: To microwave the potatoes, scrub them under cold water. Pierce all over with a fork. Microwave on high for 6 minutes. Let cool slightly. Remove skin and discard. Mash sweet potatoes with a fork. Season to taste with salt and pepper.

2 medium sweet potatoes

4 whole grain flour tortillas

1 tablespoon olive oil

1 small yellow onion, finely diced

2 cloves garlic, minced

½ teaspoon salt, plus more to taste

¼ teaspoon pepper, plus more to taste

1 teaspoon smoked paprika

1 teaspoon chili powder (or chipotle chili powder)

1 (15-ounce) can black beans, rinsed and drained

¼ cup water

½ cup salsa, such as Newman's Own mild salsa, or homemade

Optional toppings: plain Greek yogurt, chopped cilantro, shredded cheddar cheese

MY FAVORITE EGG SANDWICH

MAKES 1 SANDWICH

There's not much I love more than starting the day with an egg sandwich. If I am in a rush, I keep it simple—a scrambled egg or two on a toasted whole-grain English muffin. I just wrap it in foil and take off. But when I have time, this sandwich makes my day.

1 whole-grain English muffin
½ teaspoon olive oil
1 egg
½ tablespoon butter
Handful of fresh baby spinach
1 slice ripe tomato
2 slices ripe avocado
Splash of Sriracha (optional)

1. Toast English muffin in a toaster or countertop oven.

2. While it is toasting, heat a small nonstick skillet over medium heat. Add olive oil. When oil is warm, crack egg into the pan and cook until the egg white is fully set and the yolk is as firm as you like it, 2 to 4 minutes.

3. Plate the toasted English muffin and brush each side with butter. Top with spinach, tomato, avocado, and egg. Add Sriracha if you like it spicy. Top with other muffin half.

SPICY QUINOA BREAKFAST BOWL

SERVES 4

I taught this recipe to a group of physicians at a wellness retreat. Some of their children were there, and I brought the kids up to the demonstration table to help me out. It was amazing to see young kids so excited about a quinoa bowl for breakfast! Their parents were astonished.

1. Heat sesame oil in a large skillet over medium heat. Add scallions and ginger, and cook until fragrant, about 2 minutes. Add mushrooms and sauté until soft, about 5 minutes.

2. Combine quinoa and miso-paste mixture in a bowl, stirring to combine well. Add quinoa to mushroom mixture and cook, undisturbed, until quinoa is brown and a little crispy, 3 to 4 minutes.

3. Stir in kale or Swiss chard until wilted.

4. Stir in eggs and cook until eggs are set.

5. Divide into bowls and drizzle with garlic chili sauce or Sriracha for those who like it spicy.

NOTE: To yield 1 cup of cooked quinoa, combine ⅓ cup dried quinoa with ⅔ cup water in a small pot. Bring to a boil. Reduce heat, cover with lid, and simmer for about 15 minutes.

1 tablespoon sesame oil

3 scallions, sliced

1 teaspoon minced fresh ginger

1 cup sliced cremini mushrooms

1 cup cooked quinoa (see note)

2 teaspoons miso paste, mixed with 2 tablespoons hot water

1 cup kale or Swiss chard, chopped

2 eggs, whisked

1 teaspoon garlic chili sauce or Sriracha

SNACKS
BRIDGING THE GAP

The way our lives are set up, most of us have a long time between lunch and dinner. With lunchtime typically around noon and dinner after six, we can count on hunger striking somewhere in between. We usually need something on the fly, but who has time for a relaxing snack break?

Food companies have capitalized on this dilemma. They appeal to our love of immediate gratification by putting salty, crunchy, crispy, or sweet snacks in beautiful little packages. These packages fit perfectly in vending machines, on racks in snack bars, or in baskets at a cafeteria checkout counter. The companies' health claims make us feel good about buying them. How easy! In no time at all, you can enjoy a chocolate-covered protein bar, crispy baked chips, or crunchy, spicy orange puffs that are chemically engineered to be irresistible. For the kiddos, there are adorable little goldfish-shaped crackers, veggie chips, and gummy fruit snacks that might let you think you are offering something nutritious.

These processed snack items might be colorful and tasty, but they have way too much of what we don't need: salt, fat, and sugar; preservatives; artificial colors and flavors. They lack what our bodies really need between meals: nutrients! We—and our children—need vitamins, minerals, fiber, and phytochemicals. We need fruits and vegetables. We need good proteins and healthy fats. It is hard to get these from chemically made products that can travel long distances and have an unnaturally long shelf life.

So how do we manage our afternoon hunger without sabotaging our good health?

This collection of snack ideas is meant to help you think about afternoon eating a little bit differently. Do your best to avoid snacks in bags and boxes. Pack something ahead so you aren't stuck at the vending machine. Focus on nutrients, not just convenience. Don't shy away from nuts and healthy fats. Cut up more vegetables and fruits. Invest in some new to-go containers. Cut up a few apples. Slice up a yellow pepper. Pack a bag of nuts and toss in a few dark chocolate chips. You get the idea!

The solution to those afternoon hunger pangs is easier than you think. You will be amazed at how just a little bit of thought and preparation can transform snack time.

APPLES & PEANUT BUTTER

SERVES 2

I love apples and peanut butter as a snack, and I serve them all the time to my kids. I love how a snappy, crisp apple pairs with creamy, salty peanut butter. And as nutrition goes, the duo can't be beat. This snack offers fiber, protein, a fruit serving, and heart-healthy oils from peanuts. Best of all, it keeps everyone full and happy until dinner.

1. Slice apples and divide onto 2 plates.

2. Divide peanut butter into 2 small bowls and serve alongside the apple slices.

2 apples, one red and one green

4 tablespoons all-natural peanut butter (almond butter, cashew butter, and sunflower seed butter are also great choices)

FRESHLY POPPED POPCORN

SERVES 4 | 1 LARGE BOWL FOR SHARING

Making your own popcorn on the stovetop is fun and easy. This is such a great after-school snack—always a crowd pleaser and much healthier than microwave popcorn or the prepackaged varieties. It is also a snack kids can make themselves. The more they can do in the kitchen, the better!

3 tablespoons avocado oil, peanut oil, or canola oil (any high-temperature cooking oil)

½ cup popcorn kernels, such as Orville Redenbacher's® or Rancho Gordo®

¼ to ½ teaspoon kosher salt

1. Heat oil in a medium saucepan over medium-high heat. When oil is shimmering, add popcorn kernels in a single layer.

2. Cover the saucepan. When popping starts, hold the lid on with a slight opening to vent the steam. Shake pan occasionally. When popping slows down, after about 2 minutes, remove from heat.

3. Pour into a large serving bowl and season with salt.

FLAVOR YOUR OWN!

Here are some fun and tasty things to add to your fresh popcorn:

- 1 tablespoon nutritional yeast—this delicious vegan option tastes like Parmesan cheese

- 1 tablespoon freshly grated Parmesan cheese

- 1 tablespoon melted butter

- 1 tablespoon cinnamon mixed with 2 teaspoons sugar

EDAMAME BEANS

SERVES 4-6

I had never even heard of these until I went to a Korean restaurant during medical school. They are the perfect appetizer—snappy, salty, and delicious. And now, my kids love them. You can find these in almost any supermarket in the frozen section. They are great to have on hand. And while these are often served at dinner, they make a perfect snack. They cook up quickly and are a great, filling veggie serving—and so fun to eat! The kids love to pop the beans out of the pod.

1. Bring about 2 inches of water to a boil in a heavy-bottomed saucepan. Add the edamame. Reduce heat slightly and cook until bright green, 3 to 5 minutes.

2. Drain water thoroughly. Sprinkle with kosher salt and serve with an extra bowl for the empty pods.

1 bag frozen edamame beans, in shells

2 generous pinches kosher salt, plus more to taste

MINESTRONE

SERVES 8

You might think this soup belongs in the soup section. But no! This is, hands down, one of my favorite snacks ever. For me, it is the perfect 3 p.m. hunger buster. For my kids, minestrone is a delicious, hearty snack that nourishes them for whatever comes next—homework, soccer practice, helping me fold laundry. (OK, maybe not the last one, but I keep hoping!)

Don't be intimidated by the long ingredient list. You'll be surprised by how much of this you undoubtedly already have in your pantry. This recipe is also very flexible. You can use whatever vegetables you have on hand.

3 strips bacon, chopped

1 yellow onion, diced

2 large carrots, diced

3 stalks celery, diced

2 cloves garlic, minced

½ teaspoon salt, plus additional to taste

¼ teaspoon pepper, plus additional to taste

1 teaspoon dried oregano

1 tablespoon chopped fresh rosemary

1 russet potato, peeled and diced

1 (14.5-ounce) can diced tomatoes, juices reserved

4 cups chicken broth

2 cups water

1 (15-ounce) can cannellini beans, rinsed and drained

Salt and pepper, to taste

2 cups packed fresh baby spinach or kale

2 cups alphabet pasta or ditalini pasta

1 tablespoon olive oil

Parmesan cheese, freshly grated, for garnish

1. Heat a large soup pot or Dutch oven over medium heat. Add chopped bacon and cook until crispy, 10 to 12 minutes. Remove bacon with a slotted spoon and place on a plate lined with a paper towel.

2. Keeping the heat on medium, add onion, carrots, and celery to the pot, and cook, stirring often, until softened, about 7 minutes. Stir in garlic, salt, pepper, oregano, and rosemary; cook for 1 minute, until garlic is fragrant.

3. Stir in potato, tomatoes, broth, and water; bring to a boil. Reduce heat and simmer over low heat for 30 minutes. Add beans and greens, and continue to simmer 20 to 30 minutes longer. Season with salt and pepper. Taste and add more seasonings if needed.

4. Just before the soup is ready, bring a saucepan three-fourths full of salted water to a boil. Add pasta, stir well, and cook until al dente, according to the package instructions. Drain well and drizzle with olive oil; divide among soup bowls. Ladle the soup over the pasta, top with crispy bacon, sprinkle generously with grated cheese and serve.

READY FOR ANYTHING!

These are my essential pantry items for pulling a soup together:

- Boxed stock or stock concentrate, such as reduced-sodium Better Than Bouillon®

- Canned beans: white beans, pinto beans, and black beans, organic if possible

- Canned or boxed diced tomatoes, organic if possible

And if you keep onions, carrots, and celery on hand, you always have the foundation for a fabulous soup.

Once you have the technique down, you can adapt the recipe to use whatever vegetables, beans, and greens you have in the house.

LEMONY LENTIL HUMMUS

SERVES 4-6

I am not the kind of person who has happy kitchen accidents. Most of my accidents in the kitchen involve smoke alarms, ruined pans, and delivery pizza. This recipe is the one exception.

How did it happen? I completely overcooked some red lentils and was surprised to see that they had turned a lovely yellow. When I tried to stir them, they totally fell apart. Sigh. But I couldn't throw them out; I am way too frugal for that.

Somehow I thought to blend them with olive oil, lemon, and garlic. Voila! One of our favorite family snacks was born. It tastes great on freshly cut vegetables or whole-wheat pita chips.

1 cup red lentils

4 tablespoons olive oil

1 tablespoon tahini

Juice of 2 lemons, more to taste

2 cloves garlic, peeled

½ teaspoon kosher salt

¼ teaspoon freshly ground black pepper

1 teaspoon olive oil, for garnish

Dash of smoked (or regular) paprika, for garnish

1. Put lentils in a heavy-bottomed saucepan and cover with water by about 2 inches. Bring to a boil and stir.

2. Turn heat down to medium low, and simmer, stirring frequently, until lentils are yellow in color and fall apart when stirred, 25 to 30 minutes. Drain excess water and let cool.

3. In a food processor or high-powered blender, blend lentils, olive oil, tahini, lemon juice, garlic, salt, and pepper. Taste and adjust seasonings and consistency to your liking. For a smoother or creamier consistency, add a tablespoon or two of water to thin out the hummus. Taste and adjust seasonings.

4. Serve in a bowl and garnish with olive oil and a dash of paprika.

CARROT GINGER MUFFINS

MAKES 12 MUFFINS

This recipe is for lovers of carrot cake, for people whose crisper drawer is overflowing with carrots, or for those of us who can't get enough ginger in our lives. It's a delicious breakfast or snack, filled with whole grains and veggies, and surprisingly low in sugar.

And don't let me hold you back. Add as much ginger as you like.

2 eggs

½ cup avocado oil

¼ cup plain whole-milk yogurt

2 teaspoons vanilla extract

½ cup brown sugar

½ cup milk

1¾ cups whole-wheat pastry flour

½ cup oat flour

1 teaspoon baking powder

½ teaspoon baking soda

1 teaspoon cinnamon

2 tablespoons minced fresh ginger

½ teaspoon kosher salt

2 cups grated carrots

1. Preheat oven to 350°F. Line muffin tins with parchment or foil liners.

2. Whisk together eggs, oil, yogurt, vanilla, brown sugar, and milk in a large mixing bowl. Set aside.

3. In a medium bowl, whisk together whole-wheat pastry flour, oat flour, baking powder, baking soda, cinnamon, ginger, and salt.

4. Gradually stir the dry ingredients into the wet ingredients until blended. Do not overmix. Gently fold in grated carrot.

5. Fill muffin cups almost all the way full. Bake until a toothpick inserted in the middle comes out clean, 22 to 25 minutes.

PICKLE PLATTER

SERVES 4-6

Don't forget that pickles are awesome snacks! They have a fabulous snappy, salty appeal and are much better for you than a bag of chips. Pickles in all shapes and sizes pair well with some or all of the ingredients in the list.

Arrange pickles and other items on a cutting board, platter, or individual plates. Set out just before kids come in the door after school.

Sliced cheddar cheese
Whole-grain crackers
Olives of any size and color
Apple slices
Roasted cashews
Goat cheese
Pita chips
Salami slices
Rye or pumpernickel bread slices
Sliced red or yellow pepper

ALL ABOUT NUTS

One of the most exciting shifts in the nutrition world has been back toward the regular consumption of nuts. There was a time when nuts were out of favor for their high fat and calorie content. But a tremendous amount of research has shown that eating nuts offers many significant health benefits. The fat in nuts—unsaturated fats and omega-3 fatty acids—actually promote heart health. Nuts help you feel full and keep blood sugars stable. And nuts can help promote a stable weight.

Eating an ounce of nuts each day can be great for you. There are a lot to choose from: peanuts, cashews, almonds, pecans, and walnuts are all widely available. Don't forget nut butters; along with peanut butter, you'll see jars of almond butter and cashew butter on grocery shelves. Seeds have similar health benefits to nuts and also come in a wide variety. You can find pumpkin, chia, sunflower, and flax seeds, as well as sunflower seed butter, in most grocery stores. Nuts and seeds are perfect to include at snack time, as they help tame afternoon hunger with the fiber, protein, and nutrients we all need.

Selecting nuts and nut butters can be tricky, because of all the options available. These simple guidelines will help steer you in the right direction:

Nuts are most nutritious in their whole and raw form. Processing nuts, just like processing grains, can strip them of some of their important health benefits. Select nuts that are raw or simply dry roasted, instead of those with a lot of added salt or sugar (honey-roasted peanuts, for example).

The healthiest nut butters have the fewest ingredients—just nuts and a bit of salt. Try to avoid nut butters that have added sugars or hydrogenated oils. Look for an "all-natural" peanut butter or almond butter, and don't be put off by nut butters that need to be stirred. The oils that naturally separate are a sign that they are good for you. Stirring peanut butter can be messy but is definitely worth the effort. There are some differences between nuts in terms of how much of each kind of fat they have. Don't worry too much about that, especially if you're eating a variety of nuts and seeds.

Nuts and seeds also add flavor and texture to dishes. You will find them in various recipes throughout the book—in granola, on yogurt, on salads, and even on apple crisp. They are a great way to make your family diet more delicious and nutritious!

PISTACHIOS & CANTELOUPE

SERVES 4-6

Nuts and fruit are the perfect combination of flavor and nutrients. Nuts are rich with vitamins, minerals, and healthy fats. Fruit has natural sweetness and lots of vitamins and fiber.

1. Slice melon in half through the middle, not end to end. Scoop out seeds.

2. Lay each half down flat on a cutting board. Starting at the top, cut the rind off the flesh by moving your knife down the edge in strips. Cut around the melon until all rind is removed.

3. Cut melon into ½-inch slices and serve alongside a dish of nuts.

NOTE: You can get precut cantaloupe in the produce section or cut your own. It takes a little practice but gives you a lot more for your money.

1 cantaloupe (see note)

1 cup pistachios, shells on or off

TRAIL MIX

SERVES 4

This snack has saved me many times on busy workdays. Not only does it give me great energy for my last few patients, it also prevents me from being ravenous and cranky when I get home to my family. And don't forget: dark chocolate is good for you!

1. Heat oven to 250°F.

2. Spread almonds and cashews on a baking sheet. Roast until nuts are slightly brown and fragrant, 22 to 25 minutes. Sprinkle with salt while still warm. Let cool completely.

3. Mix nuts with chocolate chips and dried fruit. Store in an airtight container for up to 2 weeks.

1 cup raw, unsalted almonds

1 cup raw, unsalted cashews

¼ teaspoon salt

¼ cup dark chocolate chips, such as Ghirardelli®, over 60 percent cocoa

¼ cup dried cranberries or other dried fruit of your choice

PORCUPINE MANGO

SERVES 1, OR 2 IF YOU SHARE

My first magical mango experience happened during a tough surgery rotation. It was a cold winter, and life was a little bleak. On a rare break, my classmate Eric saw fresh mango at the salad bar and beamed with happiness. "Everyone, really, should be eating more mango," he said. He's right!

1. Rinse mango and dry thoroughly.

2. With a sharp knife, start at the top of the mango and cut down to the bottom, just around the pit. Turn the mango and repeat cutting all sides until the pit is out.

3. Lay mango slices skin-side down. Score the flesh into ½-inch cubes, still attached to the skin. Serve as is, or invert so that it looks like a porcupine.

4. Serve with a glass of milk.

NOTE: Mangoes are ripe when they give in to gentle pressure from the palm of your hand.

1 mango

WHOLE-WHEAT PITA CHIPS WITH GOAT CHEESE DIP

SERVES 6

I used to serve this at neighborhood parties, and it was always a hit. But our party-throwing seems to be on hold these days, while we all are busy driving our kids around to sports and activities. So now I make this for a snack and bring the leftovers to work.

I learned this goat cheese dip technique (and many other things) from Mark Bittman's book How to Cook Everything, *a cookbook collection necessity!*

FOR PITA CHIPS
- 3 whole-wheat pita bread rounds
- 2 tablespoons butter
- 2 tablespoons olive oil
- 1 tablespoon dried oregano
- 1 teaspoon dried chili flakes (optional)
- Kosher salt

FOR DIP
- 2 (4-ounce) logs plain goat cheese, room temperature
- ½ cup plain yogurt
- 1 tablespoon oregano or other dried herbs (an Italian blend or herbes de Provence work well)
- Kosher salt
- Freshly ground pepper, to taste

1. To make the pita chips, open pita rounds by separating them with your fingers or cutting with kitchen shears all around the edge. Cut each circle into 8 triangles and place on a baking sheet.

2. Melt butter in a heavy-bottomed saucepan over medium heat. Stir in olive oil. Brush onto pita with a pastry brush (a clean, cheap paintbrush from the hardware store is fine). Sprinkle with oregano, chili flakes, if using, and salt.

3. Broil on the top rack of your oven until crisp and golden brown, 3 to 5 minutes. Keep a close eye on them, as they can burn quickly. Let cool.

4. To make the dip, place goat cheese in a medium mixing bowl. Stir in yogurt with a fork or wire whisk until well-blended. The texture should be creamy but not too liquid. Season with dried herbs, salt, and pepper. At this stage, you can cover dip tightly with plastic wrap and refrigerate until ready to serve.

5. To serve, spoon goat cheese dip into a bowl with pita chips alongside.

WHOLE-GRAIN QUESADILLAS

SERVES 4

I try to always have some sort of tortilla on hand, so I can throw together a quesadilla for a hungry boy. I like to add beans—another pantry staple—for the extra flavor and healthy fiber. The salsa here can go inside the quesadilla or outside for dipping. You choose!

1. Put beans into a mixing bowl and mash with the back of a fork.

2. Heat a nonstick skillet over medium heat. Add a tortilla, and sprinkle with ½ cup shredded cheese.

3. When cheese starts to melt, add a layer of mashed beans. Add half of the avocado slices. Top with a spoonful or two of salsa and another tortilla.

4. When cheese is melted and the bottom tortilla is browned, flip and brown on the other side.

5. Slide the quesadilla onto a cutting board. Repeat to make a second one.

6. Cut quesadillas into triangles and serve immediately.

1 (15-ounce) can pinto beans, drained and rinsed

4 (8-inch) whole-grain tortillas

1 cup shredded cheese, such as Monterey Jack or cheddar, divided

1 avocado, sliced

Salsa

CHOCOLATE ZUCCHINI CAKE

SERVES 12

You probably know by now that I have two boys, a teen and a preteen. This means that while I love these boys dearly, I have a lot of low parenting moments. My husband and I affectionately call them "LPMs." Our life is full of them.

To get through these moments, I hang on to a few high points. One day, I offered my son a big piece of this cake while he was doing homework. I didn't mention it was full of healthy ingredients. He looked at me, wide-eyed, unable to believe his good fortune, and said, "Thank you, best Mommy in the world." And he meant it. For the moment, at least . . .

1. Preheat oven to 350°F. Grease a Bundt pan or a 9-inch round cake pan with nonstick cooking spray.

2. In a medium bowl, whisk together eggs, avocado oil, applesauce, vanilla, and sugar.

3. In a separate bowl, whisk together flour, cocoa, baking soda, baking powder, and salt.

4. Working in batches, add the dry ingredients to the wet ingredients. Mix until smooth. Gently fold in shredded zucchini. Pour the batter into the prepared pan.

5. Bake 50 to 60 minutes, until a toothpick inserted in the cake comes out clean.

6. Let cool on a wire rack at least 15 minutes, then turn out onto a cake platter. Dust with powdered sugar and serve.

3 eggs

¾ cup avocado oil

½ cup unsweetened applesauce

2 teaspoons vanilla extract

¾ cup brown sugar

2 cups whole-wheat pastry flour

1 cup dark cocoa powder (such as Valrhona® or Scharffen Berger®)

1 teaspoon baking soda

½ teaspoon baking powder

½ teaspoon kosher salt

2 cups shredded zucchini

Powdered sugar, for dusting

VEGETABLES
FROM CONCEPT TO REALITY

Don't you wish you had a nickel for every time a doctor said you should eat more vegetables? Me too.

And, to be honest, I say this a lot myself. With rare exceptions, children are eating far fewer vegetables than they need for good health. It is the one enduring truth of all dietary research and trends: Plants make us healthy. Regardless of the variety, plants' richness in vitamins, phytochemicals, and fiber gives us more health and disease prevention than you could ever buy in a box. The more plants we eat, the better!

But while "Eat more vegetables!" is sound, well-intentioned advice, it doesn't help you really make it happen. We all know we should be eating more vegetables—but how?

This chapter gives you the tools to put that good advice into everyday practice. These recipes and techniques will help you develop approachable, unfussy ways to get a variety of simple, delicious vegetables into your daily life. Eating more vegetables does not need to be a fancy undertaking.

But first, I want you to remember that vegetables are living things and need care. They must be washed and stored properly. They need to be sliced or diced and served in order to be eaten. They take a little work and will spoil if not used. What makes them healthy also makes them perishable; that is part of the nourishing nature of vegetables. Don't be put off by the work they require. Embrace it and enjoy the benefits!

In the pages that follow, I will highlight a range of simple techniques that will help you bring great flavor and nutrition to your table. Whether it is a side dish of raw veggies, a tasty Thai salad, steamed green beans, or a tray of spicy roasted cauliflower, all of these are made with techniques that are easy and adaptable.

Yes, you should eat more vegetables. Here's how!

VINAIGRETTE
MAKES 1 CUP

For this basic dressing, I start with olive oil and pair it with a light, snappy vinegar. Since I can't resist a beautiful bottle of citrus-infused oil, I often have flavored oil on hand. I love blood orange olive oil, which I get in the Ferry Building in San Francisco.

Making vinaigrette is a great technique to master. You have control over the flavor and ingredients, and it will always be fresher and healthier than a premade dressing. The flavor combinations are endless. You can add a teaspoon of lemon or lime zest to give it bright flavor. Or you can add a pinch of dried herbs, like oregano or basil. Master the basic recipe and adapt it as you like.

When making a dressing, the concept of taste-adjust is critical. The flavor of each vinaigrette will vary widely according to the kind of oil and vinegar you are using. Always taste the dressing first. Add more salt and pepper if needed. If it tastes flat, add a little more vinegar. If it is too tart, add more oil. Keep tasting, shaking, adjusting, and tasting—you'll get it right!

¾ cup extra-virgin olive oil or blood orange olive oil

¼ cup champagne vinegar, plus more to taste

½ teaspoon Dijon mustard

2 generous pinches kosher salt

2 grinds freshly ground black pepper

½ teaspoon sugar (optional)

1. Place oil, vinegar, mustard, salt, and pepper in a jar with a tight-fitting lid. Shake vigorously for 10 seconds or more.

2. Taste it. If it tastes sour at all, add a little sugar and taste again. Sugar helps neutralize the vinegar, which sometimes has a bite to it or might even make you cough.

3. Vinaigrette can be kept in a jar in the refrigerator up to 2 months. Just shake again prior to using, taste, and adjust, if needed.

NOTE: Infused olive oils are becoming more widely available. Blood orange, lemon, and lime are my favorites, but check your market to see what's offered.

AMY SALAD

SERVES 12

My dear friend Amy loves salad and is great about getting it on her table every night. Her go-to version is a green salad with chopped apple and walnuts. Not only do I love this salad but it also reminds me of all the laughter-filled dinners we have had together.

Be sure to set aside some of the glazed walnuts. They make a great afternoon snack.

1. Line a plate with parchment paper.

2. Combine walnuts, oil, and maple syrup in a small bowl; toss to evenly coat. Place nut mixture in a large nonstick skillet over medium heat. Cook, stirring frequently, as the syrup caramelizes and nuts become fragrant, 3 to 5 minutes. Transfer to the plate lined with parchment paper and add salt. Let cool.

3. Make the dressing: place vinegar, oil, mustard, salt, and pepper in a jar with a tight-fitting lid. Shake vigorously.

4. Toss greens, apple, onion, and cranberries in a wooden salad bowl. Dress lightly so that all leaves are glistening but no dressing pools at the bottom of the bowl.

5. Top with as many of the maple-glazed nuts as you wish, reserving any extra for a snack later. The nuts keep well in an airtight container for up to 2 weeks.

MAKE IT A MEAL!

This salad is a great base and can easily be transformed into a hearty dinner. You can add some blue cheese, some sliced grilled chicken—or both.

And if time is short, you can substitute plain chopped nuts for the maple-glazed nuts. Chopped pecans would be great too.

Remember, use what you have. These recipes are meant to be flexible!

1½ cups chopped walnuts

1 tablespoon coconut oil, walnut oil, or extra-virgin olive oil

3 tablespoons pure maple syrup

⅛ teaspoon kosher salt

FOR DRESSING

2 tablespoons apple cider vinegar

4 tablespoons extra-virgin olive oil or walnut oil

½ teaspoon Dijon mustard

Kosher salt

Freshly ground pepper, to taste

1 (5-ounce) package mixed greens, washed and thoroughly dried

1 green apple, diced

¼ red onion, sliced very thinly

¼ cup dried cranberries

GREEK SALAD
SERVES 4

This is my favorite salad to make when I come home from a business trip. When I'm not eating well on the road, I crave a big bowl of this crispy, tangy salad. It hits the spot every time.

For people (OK, usually kids) who don't like different foods touching each other on the plate, you can place some cucumbers, cherry tomatoes, and olives in individual ramekins and serve them that way. Don't worry if your kids don't like things mixed together. Someday, they will!

For everyone else, this makes a delicious mixed salad, especially when accompanied by a loaf of warm whole-grain bread.

1. Toss lettuce, cucumber, cherry tomatoes, onion, and olives in a large mixing bowl.

2. In a small jar, combine vinegar, oil, mustard, oregano, a pinch of salt, and a couple grinds of pepper, and shake vigorously. Taste and adjust seasonings by adding more salt, pepper, or vinegar as you see fit. If it tastes too sour or acidic, add sugar, shake well, and taste again.

3. Toss the salad with enough dressing to coat all the vegetables without having any liquid pooling at the bottom of the bowl.

4. Serve salad on individual plates or bowls. Top with feta cheese and serve.

---

1 head romaine lettuce, washed, dried well, and torn into bite-size pieces

1 cucumber, peeled, sliced in half lengthwise, seeded, and cut into half-moons

½ pint cherry tomatoes, halved

¼ small red onion, very thinly sliced

½ cup Kalamata olives, pitted

6 ounces feta cheese

FOR DRESSING

2 tablespoons red wine vinegar, or more to taste

¼ cup olive oil

½ teaspoon Dijon mustard

1 teaspoon dried oregano

Kosher salt

Freshly ground black pepper, to taste

¼ teaspoon sugar (optional)

CHEF'S TIP

Thick slices of raw red onion can be a little overwhelming in a salad. The first thing to do with onion is make sure to slice it as thinly as possible. If you happen to have a mandoline, this is a perfect use for it. If not, a sharp chef's knife works well too.

To finely slice red onion, cut off the root and tip. Cut in half from top to bottom (where you just cut off the root and tip). Remove papery skins from onion and discard.

Place the onion half flat-side down. Slice thinly from the tip end to root end (top to bottom).

You can also use pickled red onion in this recipe. That technique is found on page 73.

KID-FRIENDLY KALE SALAD

SERVES 6 AS A SIDE DISH, 4 AS A MAIN

I have made so many terrible kale dishes—burned kale chips, chewy and bitter kale salads . . . really awful dishes. But I didn't want to give up. Kale is incredibly good for you, and I always want to eat more dark, leafy greens.

Thankfully, going to culinary school has given me fabulous friends I can call on in moments of kitchen weakness. For this one I turned to Ellen, a great chef and a true lover of kale salad. The base of this recipe is hers. I added the couscous and grated carrot. Finally, a kale salad we all really like!

Leftovers make a terrific lunch. This salad is even better the next day.

1 bunch lacinato kale, tough stems removed, leaves chopped (about 6 cups)

½ teaspoon salt, divided

2 tablespoons freshly squeezed lemon juice

1½ cups water

1 cup whole-wheat couscous

1 carrot, grated

½ cup dried cranberries

¼ cup chopped pecans, for topping (optional)

FOR DRESSING

2 tablespoons balsamic vinegar

1 tablespoon pure maple syrup

½ teaspoon Dijon mustard

¼ cup extra-virgin olive oil

Pinch salt, plus more, to taste

Freshly ground black pepper, to taste

1. Place kale in a large mixing bowl. Sprinkle with ¼ teaspoon salt and lemon juice. With your hands, massage salt and lemon juice into kale leaves until soft, 1 to 2 minutes. Set aside.

2. In a medium saucepan, boil water with remaining ¼ teaspoon salt. Stir in couscous and bring to a boil again. Reduce heat to low and simmer, covered, 10 minutes. Remove from heat and let sit 2 to 3 minutes. Fluff with a fork.

3. To make the dressing, in a separate bowl, whisk together balsamic vinegar, maple syrup, mustard, olive oil, salt, and pepper. Taste and adjust seasonings.

4. Add couscous and carrot to kale. Stir to combine. Add dressing and mix thoroughly. Stir in dried cranberries and top with chopped pecans, if using.

ROMAINE SALAD WITH AVOCADO & POMEGRANATE SEEDS

SERVES 8

My children were never very interested in salad until we moved to California. We were stopping in on a new friend and saw a tree we didn't recognize. My son's new friend plucked an oddly shaped fruit off the tree and offered it to him. It was a pomegranate. My son was enchanted by the jewel-toned seeds inside—they were both sweet and tart. I put them in a salad, and my kids were sold! They have eaten salad ever since.

FOR DRESSING

3 tablespoons olive oil

1 tablespoon champagne vinegar, plus more to taste

¼ teaspoon Dijon mustard

Pinch kosher salt

Pinch freshly ground black pepper

1 head romaine lettuce, outer leaves removed, leaves chopped, washed in cold water and dried thoroughly (about 6 cups)

¼ cup pomegranate seeds (see note page 72)

¼ cup Toasted Pine Nuts (page 136)

1 ripe avocado, peeled and sliced

1. Measure olive oil, vinegar, mustard, salt, and pepper into a jar with a tight-fitting lid. Shake vigorously until all the ingredients are combined. Taste and adjust seasoning.

2. Toss lettuce with dressing until lettuce is evenly coated. Transfer to a serving platter or bowl.

3. Top with pomegranate seeds, pine nuts, and avocado slices. Drizzle with a bit more dressing, if desired.

4. Serve immediately.

KEY TECHNIQUE
HOW TO SEED A POMEGRANATE

You can buy pomegranate seeds—or arils—in the produce section of the supermarket. But they are better when the fruit is in season and you seed them yourself. Pomegranate juice can stain, but this technique is the easiest (and cleanest) I have tried.

Roll the pomegranate on the counter to loosen the seeds. Score the skin by running a knife around the middle of the fruit without cutting through the fruit. Pull the fruit apart into two halves. (This allows you to halve the fruit without cutting the arils.)

Hold the first half over a bowl and tap the fruit with the back of a wooden spoon. The seeds will release into the bowl as you tap on all sides of the fruit. Continue tapping until all the seeds are released. Repeat with the second half of the pomegranate.

MANGO-CELERY SALAD WITH PICKLED RED ONION & LIME VINAIGRETTE

SERVES 4-6

This salad is one of the many things in my life inspired by Comadre, a fabulous chef and my soul sister in all of life. She is amazing at taking fresh, simple ingredients and creating great flavor and texture combinations. She taught me this pairing of crisp, fresh celery and silky, succulent mango. She also taught me to pickle red onions, which are incredible on avocado toast too.

1. For pickled red onion, peel and thinly slice red onion. Place in a bowl with lime juice and zest. In a heavy-bottomed saucepan, heat water with salt and sugar, and whisk until dissolved. Pour over onion and lime juice. Allow to steep while preparing the salad.

2. For the salad, combine celery, mangoes, and avocados in a large bowl.

3. In a small bowl, whisk together lime juice, zest, olive oil, and orange juice. Salt to taste; adjust seasoning if desired.

4. Dress salad with the lime vinaigrette. Drain and rinse pickled red onion and add ¼ to ½ of the slices to the salad. Save the rest for other dishes; sprinkle on avocado toast or put inside a quesadilla. Delicious!

5. Pickled red onion can be kept in the juice, in the fridge, for up to 2 weeks.

FOR PICKLED RED ONION

½ small red onion

Juice and zest of 2 limes

1 cup water

1 tablespoon salt

1 tablespoon sugar

5 stalks celery, washed, trimmed, and thinly sliced on the bias

4 ripe mangoes, cubed

2 ripe avocados, cubed

Juice and zest of 1 lime

2 tablespoons olive oil

1 tablespoon orange juice, freshly squeezed if possible

2 pinches kosher salt

THAI CRUNCH SALAD

SERVES 4-6

One of the techniques I learned in culinary school was working with fresh herbs. They give a lively flavor to salad and other dishes. This salad pairs crunchy cabbage with the great flavors of mint and basil. If you can manage to grow these herbs in a garden or in a pot on your windowsill, you can enjoy them anytime. The fresher, the better!

This salad is delicious on its own or topped with grilled shrimp or salmon.

1. Mix together cabbage, cucumber, mint, basil, and scallions in a large bowl. Sprinkle with salt and a squeeze of lime. Set aside while you make the dressing.

2. Whisk together remaining lime juice, oil, fish sauce, mirin, chili, and honey. Taste and adjust seasonings, adding more salt if needed.

3. Toss the vegetables with the dressing. Top with chopped nuts if desired.

KEY TECHNIQUE
WORKING WITH HERBS

I learned a couple of important things about herbs in culinary school. One is that many cultures use them as a main ingredient in a salad, not just as a garnish. Also, I learned to be gentle with fresh herbs. Basil and mint in particular will bruise and discolor easily if roughly chopped.

For this salad, you can chop the herbs with a sharp chef's knife or use a technique called "chiffonade." This is done by stacking up mint or basil leaves, rolling them up lengthwise, and then slicing thinly. This results in thin ribbons, which are lovely in a salad.

Give it a try!

½ small green cabbage, thinly sliced

1 cucumber, peeled, halved lengthwise, seeded, and thinly sliced

2 heaping tablespoons chopped mint

2 heaping tablespoons chopped basil

3 scallions, light green and white parts only, thinly sliced

2 pinches kosher salt, plus more for dressing

Juice of 2 limes, divided

1 tablespoon sesame oil or avocado oil

1 tablespoon fish sauce, or more to taste

1 tablespoon mirin

1 serrano chili or Thai chili, seeds removed, diced

1 teaspoon honey

¼ cup chopped raw cashews or peanuts (optional)

ALL ABOUT
GRAINS

One of the most powerful ways of improving your diet is to improve the quality of the grains you eat. This means moving away from simple, refined grains like white flour and selecting more grains in their whole form. Whole grains such as farro, quinoa, whole wheat, steel-cut oats, and brown rice have much more nutrition to offer. Sometimes the language of grains on packages can be confusing, so keep these basics in mind:

A **WHOLE GRAIN** is the seed of a plant with all of the components of the grain intact. A grain contains three main parts: the fibrous outer coating (bran), the nutrient-rich embryo of the grain (germ), and the starchy interior (endosperm). The germ and bran are where all the fiber, protein, iron, vitamins, and nutrients are. A whole grain contains all parts of the grain and has more texture, flavor, and nutrition.

A **REFINED** or **PROCESSED GRAIN** typically has the bran and the germ removed. What is left is the fluffy, starchy element. Whole wheat, for example, is refined into white flour. White flour is what is used in bread, cereals, pasta, pizza dough, bagels, cookies, and crackers—many of the staples of our diet. The problem is these processed grains are the simple carbohydrates that tend to drive health problems like weight gain and diabetes.

There are many health benefits to eating more whole grains. Looking for the word "whole" in the ingredient list can help you find a product that contains more fiber, nutrients, and protein. Whole grains will give you a slower rise in blood sugar and keep you fuller longer. And they can be satisfying and delicious!

There are many good ways to incorporate more whole grains in your cooking. First, try starting your day with some hearty steel-cut oats. Try to bake with a variety of whole-grain flours, rather than just all-purpose flour. Experiment with whole-wheat flour, oat flour, or almond meal in your baking recipes. Instead of serving white rice and regular pasta, try some whole-wheat couscous, farro, quinoa, or brown basmati rice. They make delicious additions to lunches or dinners.

Cooking up a batch of whole grains can give you a great start to the week. Whole grains keep well and are perfect to serve in a salad, in a soup, with roasted vegetables, or topped with grilled chicken or fish.

At your next trip to the market, give some new whole grains a try. I am confident you'll be pleasantly surprised.

FARRO WITH SKILLET-ROASTED TOMATOES

SERVES 6 AS A SIDE DISH, 4 AS A MAIN

I was introduced to farro by a wonderful Mediterranean chef, Joyce Goldstein. She is one of my culinary idols. She has written many books, is an incredible chef, and is absolutely no-nonsense about how we should be feeding our families. She is still cooking and teaching in her 80s!

Farro is a terrific grain. You can cook it just like pasta, and it has a nutty flavor and texture. It holds up well in grain salads. This is one of my go-to dishes for a quick, nutritious, filling dinner that makes a perfect lunch the next day.

1. Bring water to a boil. Add salt and farro. Reduce heat and cook until farro is tender but still has a bite to the grain, 15 to 18 minutes. The best way to test for doneness is to taste.

2. While farro is cooking, heat a large skillet over medium-high heat. Add 1 tablespoon of the olive oil. Add tomatoes to pan and cook, shaking pan on occasion, until tomatoes are soft and browned on the outside, 8 to 9 minutes. Working in batches, add spinach and stir until wilted, 3 to 4 minutes.

3. Drain farro in a fine-mesh strainer. Return to warm pot and stir in remaining olive oil and lemon juice. Stir in tomatoes, spinach, salt, and a few grinds of pepper.

4. Top with goat cheese or feta cheese and serve immediately.

6 cups water

½ teaspoon salt

1½ cups farro

3 tablespoons olive oil, divided

1 pint cherry tomatoes, any color

1 (5-ounce) package baby spinach, about 4 cups

Juice of 2 lemons

Kosher salt, to taste

Freshly ground black pepper

4 ounces crumbled goat cheese or feta cheese, for topping

BENJAMIN BROCCOLI

SERVES 4-6

We have been eating broccoli this way ever since my then-seven-year-old, Benjamin, cooked it for the family. The first time he made it, his nine-year-old brother exclaimed, "This is my most favorite broccoli ever! It is better than a restaurant!"

Roasting is a key technique to learn because it can be applied to so many vegetables. Try cauliflower, asparagus, sweet potatoes—even string beans. Just adjust the time, depending on the size and thickness of the vegetable.

1 head broccoli

1 to 2 tablespoons olive oil

2 to 3 pinches kosher salt

3 grinds pepper, or more to taste

1. Preheat oven to 400°F.

2. Trim the bottom edge off broccoli and discard. Cut the stems into 2-inch pieces and cut tops into florets.

3. Arrange broccoli on a baking sheet in an even layer.

4. Drizzle broccoli with oil. Season with salt and pepper. Toss to evenly distribute oil and seasoning, and spread out evenly.

5. Roast until broccoli has some crispy, brown spots around the edges, 10 to 15 minutes.

BRAISED CARROTS

SERVES 4

1 cup water

1 pound carrots, sliced on the bias into ¼-inch pieces

¼ teaspoon kosher salt, plus more to taste

1 teaspoon brown sugar

2 teaspoons fresh minced ginger

½ tablespoon butter

2 teaspoons fresh thyme, stems removed

Braising sounds fancy, doesn't it? But actually, it isn't. It is just steaming without the steamer insert. I love how this technique gives vegetables the perfect texture. And the combination of butter, ginger, and thyme really makes these carrots sing.

Carrots are a staple for many reasons: They are inexpensive, they keep well, and almost every kid likes them. The funny thing about carrots is that most kids will like them one way or the other, raw or cooked. And siblings don't often like them the same way. No worries. That's easy to take care of. Just slice some carrots and set them aside while you cook the rest. Everyone is happy!

1. In a large sauté pan, bring water to a boil over medium-high heat. Add carrots and salt. Reduce heat to medium. Cook, stirring occasionally, until carrots are fork tender, 7 to 10 minutes..

2. Drain carrots and put back into warm pan. Stir in sugar, ginger, and butter. Garnish with thyme and serve immediately.

CORN ON THE COB

In New England, there is absolute agreement that nothing is more spectacular than fresh summer corn on the cob. We eat it voraciously when it is in season. We miss it terribly when it is not. We agree there is nothing like it.

But there is no agreement on how best to cook it. Some steam, some boil. Some put salt and sugar in the water. Some wouldn't hear of that. And some swear by putting it in the microwave, which, to me, borders on sacrilege.

I do think we can all agree on this much: Get corn at your local farmers market. Eat it as soon as possible. Don't overcook it. Roll it in butter, if that makes you happy. But perfect summer corn doesn't need anything added to be spectacular.

This is how my mom cooks it: "For a few ears, drop ears, one at a time, into boiling water, allowing the water to stay boiling. Cook just 3 minutes. Remove the corn. For lots of ears, drop them all into the boiling water, and when the water returns to a boil, in 3 to 4 minutes, the corn is done. Remove or turn off the heat, and leave the corn in a small amount of water until the rest of the food is ready."

SIMPLE STEAMED GREEN BEANS

SERVES 4-6

While we learned a lot of complicated recipes in culinary school, we also learned some incredibly simple—and invaluable—techniques. I am grateful to have learned how to treat vegetables properly and to bring out their best flavor. So many vegetables are perfect and delicious simply by steaming them for a few minutes.

A great complement is just a touch of butter and a sprinkle of salt. No fussy hollandaise sauce needed!

1 pound green beans, trimmed

⅛ teaspoon kosher salt

A grind or two of black pepper

½ tablespoon butter

1. Place a heavy-bottomed saucepan with a few inches of water over high heat. Put in a steamer insert (either a basket steamer or an insert works well). Add beans. When the water boils, turn the heat down to medium to maintain a gentle boil.

2. Steam for about 7 minutes or until beans reach your desired level of tenderness. The best way to test for doneness is to taste.

3. Top with salt, pepper, and butter and serve immediately.

FULL STEAM AHEAD

Carrots also cook up well in the steamer. Either slice them into thin rounds (¼ inch or less) or cut them into matchsticks.

Steamed broccoli is a great go-to as well. Steaming gives a nice tenderness to broccoli, which makes it a suitable finger food for little ones. Steamed broccoli with a squeeze of lemon juice is fantastic as a side dish or to stir into rice or pasta for lunch the next day.

Steamed veggies are also a terrific leftover to put into salads. They go well in a grain salad, like the Kid-Friendly Kale Salad (page 70).

SUMMER CORN SALAD

SERVES 4

This recipe was inspired by my grandmother. We spent a lot of time together in the summers, and we loved going to the farm stand to pick out corn for dinner. She taught me how to pull back a little bit of the husk and check to make sure the kernels were plump, shiny, and firm. She checked every ear to be sure each one was perfect.

She always bought extra so we could make "fried" corn the next day. She would sauté it until it was brown, crispy, and delicious. Making this always brings back those great summer memories!

1. Cut the corn off the cob by holding it upright and slicing top (the tassel end) to bottom with a sharp knife. Be sure to hold it firmly at the top with your non-cutting hand so you don't cut yourself. Slice on all sides until all the kernels are removed.

2. Heat 1 tablespoon of olive oil in a sauté pan over medium-high heat. Add corn and cook, stirring frequently, until corn is golden brown, about 6 minutes.

3. Stir together corn, avocado, and tomatoes in a serving bowl. Drizzle with remaining olive oil, lime juice, cilantro, salt, and pepper. Taste, adjust seasonings, and serve.

NOTE: You also can substitute about 3 cups of leftover cooked corn; frozen corn is also fine.

4 ears husked corn (see note)

2 tablespoons olive oil, divided

1 ripe avocado, cubed

1 pint cherry tomatoes, quartered

Juice of 1 lime

2 tablespoons chopped cilantro

Kosher salt, to taste

Freshly ground pepper, to taste

SOUPS, STEWS, & MAKE-AHEADS

STRATEGIES FOR SANITY

For a mother of rambunctious boys, an email from the teacher is always a little unnerving.

Especially when the title is "Your son at lunch." It is a safe bet that it is not good news. I dread these kinds of emails.

But on the day I sent my second-grader to school with a thermos full of his favorite soup, I was in for a pleasant surprise. The email—which I still have—read:

re: Your son at lunch

Dear Mrs. Nordgren,

Today at lunch when your son opened his soup, it filled the classroom with an amazing aroma. Everyone wanted to know what kind of soup it was, and if they could try it! Andrew said you made it from scratch.

Is there any chance you would be willing to share the recipe with our class?

We would appreciate it!

Mrs. G

From then on, I was known as the Soup Mom. I carried this title proudly all through the boys' elementary school years. Since I would never be Volunteer of the Month or Parent of the Year, I took whatever title I could get!

Truth be told, my habit of sending the kids to school with soup was born out of my poor shopping and planning skills. I've spent many weekend afternoons pulling out vagrant vegetables from the back of the crisper drawer, or figuring out what on earth to do with a quarter cup of brown rice and seven cans of garbanzo beans.

Soup is the age-old, tried-and-true way to put misfit ingredients to good use and to create bowls of nourishing deliciousness out of hardly anything at all. Soup is so flexible; it can be pulled together in a few minutes or left to simmer on the stove for hours. It can be assembled in the morning and hang out in the crockpot until dinnertime. Leftovers can be frozen in zip-close bags; that way a healthy, hearty meal is on deck for whenever you need it most.

All of these recipes—for soups, stews, and dishes you can make ahead—put great flavor and nourishment on your table. They make wonderful dinners and reheat beautifully for lunch the next day. Pack some to go and, who knows, you might become famous to a room full of seven-year-olds!

BRAZILIAN CHICKEN & RICE SOUP

SERVES 4

There is nothing more comforting than a bowl of chicken and rice soup. This is far and away my kids' favorite, and it's a fantastic recipe to make on a weekend afternoon. It yields enough chicken to use in the soup, with extra meat to save for later. Cooked chicken is good to have on hand to wrap in a burrito or to top a kale salad.

Like many families, I have one child who likes things mild, and one who enjoys some spice. I solve this by serving hot sauce or Sriracha on the side. The spice lovers can add as much as they like.

1. Rinse chicken pieces, place in a large stockpot, and cover with cold water by about an inch. Bring to a boil and then turn down to a simmer. You should see bubbles popping around the edge of the pot, but it should not be vigorously boiling.

2. As the stock simmers, foam will rise to the top. Using a spoon or a small strainer, skim the foam off the stock occasionally as it simmers.

3. After about 30 minutes of simmering, add onion, carrots, celery, garlic, parsley stems, thyme, peppercorns, and salt.

4. Allow to simmer for about 1 hour and 45 minutes. Remove chicken and let it cool on a cutting board. When cool, pull the meat off the bones with your fingers and set aside. Discard the skin.

5. Taste the broth. If it tastes weak, add chicken bones back in and simmer for another hour. Season with salt and pepper as needed.

1 whole organic chicken, about 4 pounds, cut into pieces

FOR THE STOCK

1 onion, cut into quarters (not peeled)

2 carrots, coarsely chopped

3 stalks celery, coarsely chopped

1 bunch parsley stems (leaves chopped and reserved for garnish)

3 cloves garlic, peeled and sliced

5 to 6 sprigs thyme

1 tablespoon whole peppercorns

1 teaspoon kosher salt, plus more, to taste

FOR THE SOUP

2 cups cooked brown rice

3 scallions, white and light green parts only, thinly sliced

2 carrots, grated

½ yellow onion, grated or finely diced

3 plum tomatoes, seeds removed, diced

Lemon wedges, for serving

Hot sauce or Sriracha, for serving (optional)

6. If it is flavorful enough for you, go ahead and strain it using a cheesecloth-lined mesh strainer. Discard the vegetables.

7. Put the strained broth back into the pot. Add rice and 2 cups of the shredded chicken. Stir. Add scallions, carrots, onion, and tomatoes. Heat through, stirring occasionally, about 5 minutes.

8. Garnish with parsley leaves and serve with lemon wedges and hot sauce, if desired.

CHEF'S TIP
SHORTCUT ALERT

During a busy week, there is rarely time to make chicken stock. Don't let that stop you from enjoying this soup. For a quicker version, use premade chicken broth and precooked, shredded chicken. You can use a boxed stock like Pacific® low-sodium organic chicken broth or Swanson low-sodium chicken broth. Another option is a chicken stock concentrate such as Better Than Bouillon® roasted chicken base. Use 1 teaspoon of concentrate for each cup of water.

Then, just add the vegetables, precooked chicken, and some leftover rice. I often stick with the scallion, grated carrot, and diced tomatoes for a quick version. Easy and delicious!

ROB'S ALMOST-WORLD-FAMOUS VEGGIE CHILI

SERVES 6-8

My husband's superpower is actually doing dishes. Thank goodness! I can make a delicious meal, but I make a crazy mess in the kitchen. Every now and then, however, Rob steps out of his comfort zone and makes his chili, which is famous to us, if no one else. The boys and I happily do dishes when he does the cooking.

This chili tastes even better the next day.

1. Heat olive oil in a stockpot over medium-high heat. When oil is shimmering, add diced onion and cook, stirring, 5 to 7 minutes, until soft. Add garlic and cook 1 minute more. Add chili powder, cumin, and ancho chili powder, if using, and cook 1 minute more.

2. Stir in yellow pepper and carrots, and cook for another 5 to 7 minutes, until veggies soften a little. Add salt and pepper.

3. Add stock, chickpeas, tomatoes, and pinto beans. Bring to a boil and then turn down to a simmer. Cook, stirring occasionally, 30 minutes.

1 tablespoon olive oil

1 small yellow onion, diced

5 cloves garlic, minced

2 teaspoons chili powder

2 teaspoons cumin

1 teaspoon ancho chili powder or chipotle chili powder (optional, but adds a nice smoky flavor)

1 yellow pepper, diced

2 carrots, peeled and diced

½ teaspoon kosher salt

¼ teaspoon ground pepper

3 to 4 cups vegetable stock, depending on desired consistency

2 (15-ounce) cans chickpeas, rinsed and drained

1 (28-ounce) can diced tomatoes with juices

2 (15-ounce) cans pinto beans, rinsed and drained

ROASTED CAULIFLOWER

SERVES 4-6

At home we rely a lot on roasted vegetables during the week. We all love the flavor, and the recipe is so flexible. It's a terrific make-ahead dish. You can roast many kinds of vegetables, use any kind of spice you like, and exact timing isn't critical. And leftovers are perfect for serving with scrambled eggs or packing up for a snack at work.

Cauliflower has a mild flavor that goes well with spices. It is a great way to add color and flavor to your table. My favorites are turmeric (which has super health benefits!) and smoked paprika, which has a gorgeous color.

1. Preheat oven to 400°F.

2. Chop cauliflower into florets and arrange on a baking sheet. Use a sheet of parchment if you have it.

3. Toss with olive oil, salt, pepper, and colorful spice of choice. Spread out to form an even layer of cauliflower.

4. Roast until cauliflower is crisp and brown on the outside, 12 to 15 minutes.

5. Serve hot.

1 medium head cauliflower

1 tablespoon olive oil

¼ teaspoon kosher salt

¼ teaspoon ground black pepper

2 teaspoons turmeric or smoked paprika

ALL ABOUT
FLAVOR

One of the revelations in my culinary life has been learning the simple art of developing great flavor. Cooking something inviting and delicious—especially after a long day at work—doesn't need to be overwhelming. It also doesn't require extraordinary ingredients. With just a few key items on hand, you can re-create flavors from the Mediterranean, Asia, India, Mexico, and Thailand—no takeout necessary!

These are my absolute go-to flavor makers.

SALT. *This is essential to bring out the flavor of just about any dish. What I use in cooking is always less than what is used in packages or restaurant food. Keep a little dish of kosher salt near your stove, and get into the habit of "taste—adjust"; add a bit of salt, taste, add more if you need, taste again. A well-seasoned dish won't need any salt at the table.*

PEPPER. *Freshly ground pepper is another essential. A good pepper grinder is a great investment. You can even experiment with different colors of peppercorns. They add color and flavor to a dish.*

OLIVE OIL. *This is dear to my heart for being such a healthy, flavorful base to a mouthwatering salad dressing, a hearty pesto, or a snappy hummus. It carries flavors well and is an everyday cooking essential.*

AROMATICS. *Onion, garlic, shallots, and scallions are core flavor components of almost every meal.*

SPICES. *These are worth their weight in gold. Just a few spices can bring so many different flavors to your table. While this is by no means a complete list, these are the global items in my spice cabinet:*

- **Asian**—ground ginger, powdered garlic (when I don't have fresh), Chinese 5-spice powder, miso paste, toasted sesame oil, Sriracha
- **Indian**—cumin, cinnamon, yellow curry, garam masala, red curry paste, turmeric
- **Mexican**—chili powder, smoked paprika, chipotle chili powder, dried oregano
- **Thai**—red or green curry paste, green curry powder, lemongrass, kaffir lime leaves
- **Mediterranean**—oregano, basil, parsley, thyme, bay leaves

CITRUS. *Fresh lemons and limes brighten up just about everything. I use a lot of citrus—both juice and zest—in salad dressings, on vegetables, in marinades, and in soups. Pick up a lemon, a lime, and an orange each time you shop and keep them on your counter. Great flavor will always be in reach.*

INDIAN LENTIL SOUP
SERVES 8-10

2 tablespoons olive oil
1 small yellow onion, diced
3 ribs celery, diced
3 carrots, diced
3 cloves garlic, minced
1 tablespoon yellow curry powder
1 teaspoon cumin
1 generous pinch cayenne pepper (optional)
½ teaspoon kosher salt, plus more as needed
½ teaspoon ground black pepper
2 cups red lentils
6 cups chicken stock or vegetable stock
1 (28-ounce) can diced tomatoes with juice

FOR EACH SERVING
1 tablespoon plain Greek yogurt
1 to 2 teaspoons fresh cilantro, coarsely chopped
1 lemon wedge

Having a few soups in your repertoire is like having a secret culinary superpower. You can create a dish with amazing, complex flavor and texture from the simplest, least expensive, most nutrient-rich vegetables around. This is especially true for lentil soup. It is delicious and filled with fiber and healthy protein. Happily, my kids love it.

This soup also shows off a life-changing lesson I learned from cookbook author and friend, Mindy Fox: a generous squeeze of lemon juice brings incredible life to just about any soup. Give it a try!

1. Heat oil in a large soup pot until shimmering. Add onion, celery, and carrots and sauté, stirring frequently, until vegetables are soft, 5 to 7 minutes. Add garlic and cook 1 minute more. Add curry powder, cumin, and cayenne pepper, if using, and stir until fragrant, about 1 minute. Add salt and black pepper.

2. Stir in lentils and cook 2 minutes more.

3. Add stock and bring to a boil. Reduce heat and add tomatoes. Simmer until lentils are tender, about 30 minutes.

4. Ladle into soup bowls and garnish with yogurt, cilantro, and a generous squeeze of fresh lemon juice.

KALE AND WHITE BEAN STEW

SERVES 8

I am from New England, so I always need a few hearty stews to get me through the winter. I taught this recipe to my Dartmouth Culinary Medicine class, and it was the students' favorite meal. We made it on a cold, snowy night and it hit the spot.

1. In a large Dutch oven or soup pot, heat oil over medium-high heat. When oil is shimmering, add onion and cook until translucent, about 5 minutes. Add garlic, sage, rosemary, and/or thyme and cook 1 minute more. Add sausage, if using, and cook until meat is no longer pink, 7 to 8 minutes.

2. Add tomatoes, beans, and stock. Bring to a boil, then reduce heat and simmer for 20 minutes, or longer if you have time.

3. Add kale and allow to slightly wilt, at least 2 minutes. Season with kosher salt and pepper to taste. Divide stew among bowls and top with grated Parmesan.

1 tablespoon olive oil

1 small yellow onion, diced

2 cloves garlic, minced

1 teaspoon dried sage

1 teaspoon dried rosemary or thyme (or both)

1 pound ground hot Italian sausage (optional)

1 (14.5-ounce) can diced tomatoes

1 (15-ounce) can white beans (or 1 cup cooked white beans), drained and rinsed

5 cups chicken or vegetable stock

1 small bunch lacinato kale, washed, stems removed, leaves chopped

Kosher salt

Freshly ground black pepper

Grated Parmesan cheese, for serving

TERIYAKI MEATBALLS

MAKES 24 1-INCH MEATBALLS

1 cup breadcrumbs

¾ cup milk

2 eggs

2 pounds ground turkey or pork, or 1 pound of each

1 bunch scallions (5 or 6), white and green parts, finely chopped

2 cloves garlic, minced

¼ cup low-sodium teriyaki sauce

¼ teaspoon kosher salt

5 or 6 grinds fresh black pepper

There is something nice and approachable about a meatball. When my kids were toddlers, I liked to make the meatballs small for their little hands. I also found that roasting meatballs in the oven is much less fuss than cooking them on the stovetop (and made it easier to chase toddlers while cooking). I still prepare meatballs that way.

This recipe makes a great dinner with enough for lunch for the next day. You can also make a double batch; any meatballs you don't eat can be stored in a zip-close bag in the freezer for up to a month.

1. Preheat oven to 350°F. Line a baking sheet with parchment paper, or use one with a wire rack.

2. Combine breadcrumbs and milk in a large mixing bowl and set aside.

3. In a separate bowl, whisk eggs. Add ground meat, scallions, garlic, and teriyaki sauce. Season with salt and pepper. Add breadcrumb mixture and mix with your hands until well-combined. Be careful not to overmix or the meatballs will be tough.

4. With your hands, gently form the mixture into 1-inch balls and place on the baking sheet or wire rack.

5. Bake 20 to 22 minutes, until cooked through and browned on the outside, turning once halfway through cooking time.

CHEF'S TIP
MAKING BAKING A BREEZE

Baking sheets are the workhorses of my kitchen. I use them for everything—baking cookies, roasting vegetables, oven fries, making meatballs—you name it. I swear by lining baking sheets with parchment paper. It helps food release easily from the pan and makes cleanup much easier for the "dish team."

For each of my large baking sheets, I have a wire rack that fits perfectly. I use them in the oven for anything that will render fat, like meatballs or bacon. The fat drips through and allows for even cooking.

My favorite baking sheets and racks come from King Arthur Flour. If you are ever near Norwich, Vermont, stop by their amazing flagship store for a great foodie shopping experience!

MISO SOUP
SERVES 4

Miso is one of those magical soups that everyone seems to love. You can add tofu or not, depending on each person's preferences. Either way, this is a great start to a meal. Miso paste can be found at most major supermarkets. Look for it in the produce aisle, near the tofu.

3 tablespoons miso paste, plus more to taste

2 cups water

2 cups vegetable stock (mushroom stock works well)

1 bunch scallions, thinly sliced

8 ounces firm tofu, drained and cut into small cubes

8 ounces fresh baby spinach leaves

1. Heat miso paste, water, stock, and scallions in a soup pot until miso dissolves. Do not vigorously boil; it should be steaming but not at a rolling boil. Give it a taste: If the soup seems bland, add another tablespoon of miso.

2. Divide tofu and baby spinach into four bowls.

3. Pour hot broth into the bowls. Serve immediately.

PHO

SERVES 4

I had never tried pho before I went to culinary school. Our Cuisines of Asia class opened my eyes to this incredible soup, and I have loved it ever since. We enjoy this at home with fresh sprouts and herbs from the farmers market.

This dish calls for a few pantry items you might not have, like star anise and cloves. Adding them to your spice cabinet gives you the power to make this soup at home—you won't regret it!

1 tablespoon avocado oil or vegetable oil

1 small onion, unpeeled, cut into quarters

2 cloves garlic, crushed

1 (1-inch) piece ginger, peeled and cut into thin slices

1 (3-inch) cinnamon stick

1 whole star anise

2 whole cloves

2 cups beef stock (see Chef's Tip)

2 cups water

Kosher salt, to taste

8 ounces rice noodles

FOR GARNISH

2 cups bean sprouts

1 bunch cilantro, chopped

1 jalapeño or serrano pepper, thinly sliced

1 lime, cut into wedges

½ pound thinly sliced cooked pork tenderloin (optional)

1. Heat oil in a soup pot over medium heat. Brown onion, garlic, and ginger until caramelized on all sides. Add cinnamon, star anise, and cloves. Toast the spices, stirring once or twice, until fragrant, about 2 minutes.

2. Add stock and water. Bring to a boil; reduce heat and simmer about 10 minutes. Season to taste.

3. Discard onion, garlic, ginger, cinnamon, and star anise.

4. Add rice noodles and cook until soft, 3 to 4 minutes.

5. Ladle broth into bowls and garnish with desired toppings.

CHEF'S TIP

STOCK OPTION

Selecting a good beef broth is key to making this soup taste great. Canned beef broth can be tricky. Many varieties I have tried taste metallic or overly salty. I recommend skipping the can and selecting a boxed stock or a stock concentrate.

Currently, my favorite is Better Than Bouillon roasted beef stock concentrate. It dissolves easily in hot water and keeps well in the refrigerator between uses.

Experiment and find one you like.

THAI CHICKEN SOUP

SERVES 6

I love Thai flavors. If you live in a warm climate, this recipe is a great reason to have your own kaffir lime tree. The leaves can be used year-round to make delicious soups. If you can't find kaffir lime leaves, just substitute some fresh lime juice instead. This soup is lively, delicious, and comforting all at the same time.

1. Heat coconut oil in a soup pot over medium-high heat. Add shallots and sauté until soft, about 3 minutes. Add chili or serrano pepper, ginger, and garlic, and sauté until fragrant, about 1 minute. Add curry powder and cook another minute or so.

2. Add chicken stock, lime leaves or juice, and coconut milk. Bring to a simmer and cook about 20 minutes, while the flavors come together. Taste and adjust seasonings. Add more salt or spice as needed.

3. Stir in carrot, scallions, and chicken, and bring to a simmer again. Cook until chicken is warmed through, about 2 minutes.

4. Ladle into bowls and top with a generous sprinkling of cilantro. Serve with lime wedges.

1 tablespoon coconut oil

2 shallots, minced

1 Thai chili or serrano pepper, seeds removed, minced

1 heaping teaspoon fresh grated ginger

2 cloves garlic, minced

2 tablespoons yellow curry powder

4 cups chicken stock

3 kaffir lime leaves or 2 tablespoons fresh lime juice

1 (13.5-ounce) can coconut milk, shaken well

½ teaspoon kosher salt, plus more to taste

1 carrot, grated

3 scallions, green and white parts, thinly sliced

2 cups shredded cooked chicken

1 cup chopped cilantro, for garnish

1 lime, cut into wedges, for garnish

DINNER
MAINLY DELICIOUS

I love cooking dinner. I love the sound of diced onion hitting a hot pan. I love how stirring in spices makes the house smell amazing. Most days, cooking is a way I relax and unwind.

But I also work. I run late. I feel exhausted and depleted from a busy day. I feel weighed down by unfinished clinic notes and unanswered emails. Some days I have no energy to come up with a clever, delicious meal that pleases everyone.

Honestly, I might rely more on takeout if I were in a different line of work. But as a physician, every day I see the unintended consequences of relying on meals prepared outside the home. I see how these foods, while momentarily convenient, drive weight gain and cholesterol problems. So even when I have spent all my creative energy elsewhere, I still try to make dinner.

This is when I rely on recipes I know well. I turn to basic techniques and fresh ingredients to get something good on the table. It doesn't have to be fancy to be nourishing. Very often, the simpler, the better!

The recipes that follow are based on the foods and flavors that we know and love. You'll see some familiar favorites—tacos, stir-fry, and pasta—all with more flavor and nutrition. You will also see flavor elements of cuisine from favorite restaurants—Mexican, Indian, Asian, Mediterranean—that can easily be prepared from scratch.

The recipes I rely on, and that I want to share with you, meet a few important criteria:

FLEXIBLE. I need to be able to use what I have. I need to be able to substitute whichever veggies are on hand or the variety of beans I have in the pantry, or to add more spice if I'm in the mood. I can't be bothered by being too exact.

FORGIVING. I need my recipes to have a little wiggle room. If it cooks for 12 minutes or 16 or 20, it doesn't really matter; the dish will be fine. I need to be able to walk away for a minute or two without ruining everything.

FLAVORFUL. It has to taste good! Flavor is the key element of any good meal worth repeating. And with fresh ingredients and a well-stocked spice cabinet, a delicious dish is always within reach.

I encourage you to experiment with these recipes and adapt them to your own preferences and tastes. Don't worry about following the recipe exactly. Don't worry about screwing it up. I have no doubt it will be better than any takeout!

BREADED CHICKEN "TENDERS"

SERVES 4-6

This is a fabulous technique for any parent who wants to avoid—or get out of—the chicken nugget trap. These are infinitely healthier and far more delicious.

1. Preheat oven to 350°F. Line a baking sheet with parchment paper.

2. Prepare chicken by slicing each breast into 3 or 4 thin strips. Season with salt and pepper.

3. In a shallow bowl, combine flour, salt, and pepper. In a separate shallow bowl, whisk egg and milk. In a third shallow bowl, mix together breadcrumbs and herbs.

4. Dredge chicken strips in the seasoned flour, shaking off any excess. Dip in the egg wash, then coat with breadcrumbs.

5. When all the chicken is coated, heat 2 tablespoons of oil in a sauté pan until oil is shimmering.

6. Cook chicken in the hot oil until golden brown on both sides, 1 to 2 minutes per side. Place on prepared

1½ pounds boneless, skinless chicken breast

¼ teaspoon kosher salt

¼ teaspoon freshly ground pepper

½ cup all-purpose flour

1 egg

2 tablespoons milk

1 cup breadcrumbs (regular, whole-wheat, or panko all work well)

1 teaspoon dried oregano or Italian seasoning blend

¼ to ½ cup light oil, such as avocado, grapeseed, canola, or safflower

Lemon wedges

baking sheet and bake 10 to 15 minutes, until chicken is cooked through.

7. Serve with lemon wedges.

CHEF'S TIP

THE BEAUTY OF BREADING

This is a another great technique to have in your repertoire. You can use this breading on other lean proteins, like turkey scaloppini (thin turkey cutlets you can find in the meat section) or thin slices of pork.

It also works well with slices of eggplant or zucchini. It can be an excellent way to offer vegetables to your kids because the breading is familiar. I usually say something like, "You know the breading you like on chicken? I tried it on eggplant. Let me know what you think!" I don't make a big deal out of it either way. It is always a process to get kids to eat vegetables, but I really believe that the more ways kids have them, the better!

ANGEL HAIR PASTA

SERVES 6

The next time you are at the supermarket, check out all of the varieties of pasta available. There are so many great choices, from fabulous high-protein pastas made with plant proteins (like chickpea and soy flours) to whole-grain. These offer more nutrition than a typical semolina pasta and tend to be less starchy and more filling. Try something new—you might be surprised!

1 (14.5-ounce) box Barilla® ProteinPlus angel hair pasta or other high-protein pasta

4 tablespoons olive oil or butter, or a combination of both

Juice of one lemon

2 pinches kosher salt

1 to 2 pinches ground black pepper

1 cup chopped parsley, about ½ bunch

Grated Parmesan cheese for serving

1. Bring a large pot of salted water to a rolling boil. Drop in pasta and stir. When water boils again, turn heat to medium to maintain a boil. Cook pasta al dente, when it is soft on the outside and still has a little "bite" in the middle, about 4 minutes. Drain and set aside. Do not rinse.

2. In the pasta pot, heat oil and/or butter over medium heat. Stir in lemon juice, salt, pepper, and parsley. Cook until fragrant, about 2 minutes. Return cooked pasta to pot. Stir to coat evenly.

3. Top with freshly grated Parmesan and serve.

SIMPLE SALMON

SERVES 4

This is a go-to recipe in the middle of the week when time and energy are limited. While the salmon is cooking, steam some broccoli or cauliflower. You'll have a beautiful dinner on the table in 20 minutes.

1. Preheat oven to 400°F.

2 Place salmon on a sheet tray. Brush with oil and sprinkle with salt and pepper. Top with lemon slices.

3. Roast until salmon is a bit brown on the edges but still a bit soft in the middle, about 15 minutes. You can use a thermometer and take the fish out of the oven when the internal temperature is 140°F. Let rest 5 minutes.

4. Serve with lemon wedges, if desired.

1 to 1½ pounds salmon (wild-caught, if possible), 4 to 6 ounces per person

1 teaspoon olive oil

Kosher salt

Pepper

1 lemon, sliced

Lemon wedges for serving (optional)

CHEF'S TIP
FISH DECISIONS

There is so much to consider when choosing fish. The decision can be overwhelming. What to choose? Where is it from? How was it raised? How was it caught? All of those questions are important. The fish we eat and the way it is raised and caught has a major impact on the health of our oceans.

Thankfully, there are some great organizations committed to helping us understand how to make seafood choices. The Monterey Bay Aquarium has a Seafood Watch website where you can look up any kind of seafood and find out how to make the best choices. You can download a card to keep in your wallet.

You can also ask your fish handler. If you shop in a fish market (which I recommend if you have access to one), they will know a lot about the source of their fish.

VEGGIE STIR-FRY WITH SUPER 6 SAUCE

SERVES 4-6

When I first met my husband, he could do a few meals: takeout, tacos, and a basic stir-fry. I mean basic. He has upped his game since then in many ways. One of them is mastering the Super 6 Sauce. And as much as I love to cook, I really love it when someone else makes dinner!

The first Super 6 ingredients are the trinity of Asian flavor: ginger, garlic, and scallions. Soy, mirin, and Sriracha pull it together and add salty, sweet, and spicy elements. If I am missing an ingredient, it becomes Super 5 Sauce. No biggie—it is still delicious.

FOR SUPER 6 SAUCE

- 2 tablespoons minced ginger, divided
- 2 tablespoons minced garlic, divided
- 1 bunch scallions, light green and white parts, sliced
- ½ cup soy sauce
- 4 tablespoons mirin or rice wine vinegar, plus more to taste
- 1 heaping teaspoon Sriracha, plus more to taste

FOR STIR-FRY

- 1 tablespoon safflower oil, avocado oil, or any light vegetable oil
- 1 tablespoon toasted sesame oil
- 2 small zucchini, halved lengthwise and thinly sliced
- 3 carrots, thinly sliced
- 1 yellow onion, thinly sliced
- 2 cups cooked brown rice

1. Whisk 1 tablespoon ginger, 1 tablespoon garlic, and half the scallions with all of the soy sauce, mirin or rice wine vinegar, and Sriracha. Taste and adjust seasonings.

2. Heat vegetable oil and sesame oil in a large sauté pan or wok. When very hot, add zucchini, carrots, onion, and remaining ginger, garlic, and scallions.

3. Cook, stirring frequently, until vegetables are a bit soft but still crispy on the inside, 3 to 5 minutes. Add ¼ cup of Super 6 Sauce and stir until heated through, 1 minute.

4. Serve over rice. Serve remaining sauce at the table for those who want more.

ANDREW'S FAVORITE FAJITAS

SERVES 4

I first fell in love with fajitas growing up in New England when my high school besties—Laura, Jen, and Denise—and I would zip down Route 9 for dinner at Houlihan's. These sizzling platters of peppers, onions, chicken, and steak were the first of many great meals together!

Now, our fajita-fest tradition is a family favorite. Andrew loves them piled with grilled pineapple. Yum!

1. For the marinade, mix together Worcestershire sauce, vinegar, olive oil, chili powder, cumin, garlic, salt, and pepper in a bowl. Put flank steak in a large plastic bag and pour in the marinade. Massage the marinade into the steak so it all distributes evenly. Put in the refrigerator and marinate for at least 1 hour, and up to overnight.

2. Preheat a grill or grill pan over high heat; lightly oil grates.

3. Grill sliced pineapple for 3 to 4 minutes per side, until heated through and grill marks appear. Remove from heat. Cut into bite-size pieces.

4. Remove steak from marinade; discard excess marinade. Grill steak 5 to 7 minutes per side. Remove from heat and let rest 5 to 10 minutes.

5. Meanwhile, heat a large sauté pan over medium heat. Add olive oil and cook onion and red and yellow peppers until tender, 8 to 10 minutes. Remove from heat.

6. Slice meat thinly, against the grain, for tender slices.

7. Fill each tortilla with sautéed vegetables, a couple of slices of steak, and grilled pineapple.

OPTIONAL: Combine the adobo sauce ingredients. Top fajitas with adobo sauce for a smoky, creamy, spicy flavor.

FOR THE MARINADE

2 tablespoons Worcestershire sauce

¼ cup red wine vinegar

½ cup olive oil

1 teaspoon chili powder

1 teaspoon cumin

3 cloves garlic, minced

½ teaspoon kosher salt

½ teaspoon ground black pepper

FOR THE FAJITAS

1 pound flank steak

1 fresh pineapple, peeled, cored, and sliced, or 1 (20-ounce) can sliced pineapple

1 tablespoon olive oil

1 yellow onion, thinly sliced

1 red bell pepper, thinly sliced

1 yellow pepper, thinly sliced

8 tortillas

FOR THE ADOBO SAUCE (OPTIONAL)

½ cup plain Greek yogurt

1 to 2 tablespoons chopped chipotle chili in adobo sauce

ESSENTIAL MARINARA SAUCE

SERVES 6-8

In college, my adorable Italian professor could not understand why Americans would ever buy jarred pasta sauce. "It is so simple to make, studenti!" she said. She added in a vocabulary lesson with all the ingredients, insisting that a bit of sugar is the secret to a perfect Italian sauce.

1. Heat olive oil in a large saucepan over medium heat. Add onion. Cook until translucent, 5 to 7 minutes. Add garlic and oregano, and cook 1 minute more. Add tomatoes and season with salt, pepper, and sugar. Simmer this for a minimum of 15 minutes, and up to an hour.

2. When you are ready to serve, stir in basil and swirl in butter.

3. Serve on your favorite pasta.

Buon appetito!

1 tablespoon olive oil

1 small yellow onion, diced

3 cloves garlic, minced

1 teaspoon dried oregano

1 (28-ounce) can crushed tomatoes

1 (28-ounce) can diced tomatoes

½ teaspoon kosher salt, plus more to taste

Freshly ground pepper

½ teaspoon sugar, plus more to taste

½ cup loosely packed basil leaves, chopped

½ tablespoon butter

CAULIFLOWER TACOS

SERVES 4-6

Everyone loves tacos—for good reason! These tacos are full of flavor and have all the veggies, whole grain, and lean protein to make a nutritious meal.

- 12 (6-inch) whole-grain tortillas
- 1 tablespoon olive oil
- 1 small yellow onion, diced
- 3 cloves garlic, minced
- 2 teaspoons chili powder
- 1 teaspoon smoked paprika
- 2 cups riced cauliflower (see note below)
- ½ cup water
- 1 can black beans, drained and rinsed
- 1 can diced tomatoes, with juice
- ½ teaspoon kosher salt
- Ground pepper

SUGGESTED TOPPINGS:

- 2 cups shredded lettuce
- ½ pint quartered cherry tomatoes
- 1 cup shredded cheddar cheese
- 1 diced avocado with a big squeeze of lime juice and a sprinkle of salt
- 1 cup salsa
- A bottle of hot sauce for the table

1. Prepare all the toppings and set on the table in individual bowls.

2. Wrap the stack of tortillas in foil and put in the oven to warm while preparing the filling.

3. Heat a sauté pan over medium heat. Add oil. When oil is shimmering, add onion and sauté until translucent, about 5 minutes. Add garlic and sauté a minute more. Add chili powder and smoked paprika. Stir until fragrant, 1 to 2 minutes.

4. Add cauliflower and water. Cook, stirring occasionally, until water evaporates and cauliflower softens, about 5 minutes. Add beans, tomatoes, salt, and pepper. Stir and cook for 15 minutes, until liquid from the tomatoes evaporates and the mixture is heated through. Taste and add more salt and pepper if needed.

5. Serve the spiced beans and cauliflower mixture in warm tortillas, and allow everyone to dress them at the table.

CHEF'S TIP

RICED CAULIFLOWER

True, it isn't hard to make riced cauliflower. Just grate it on the large holes of a box grater, or pulse a few times in a food processor. Easy!

Also true, however, is that many supermarkets now carry riced cauliflower. And it is a great time-saver. It comes either fresh or frozen and both work well. Whatever it takes to get more veggies on the table!

ALL ABOUT
OILS

When someone wants to know, "What is the best cooking oil to use?" my short answer is, four of them. But the longer answer is really that oils have different uses, and a few things matter when selecting one for a particular dish.

1. FLAVOR. *A neutral oil—one that doesn't have a lot of flavor of its own—is ideal when you want the pure taste of what you are cooking to come through. A richly flavored oil like sesame oil is terrific when you want to bring that particular element to a dish. Olive oil also adds its own flavor to dressings and sauces.*

2. SMOKE POINT. *This matters a lot when you are using an oil in pans on the stovetop. A low smoke point means that the oil is likely to smoke and burn at a lower temperature. A high smoke point means that it can tolerate high heat and won't smoke until it gets extremely hot (over 500°F). Smoke point doesn't matter for a salad dressing but does for sautéing or frying.*

3. HEALTH BENEFITS. *Every oil varies in the proportion of the kinds of fats it has. Saturated fats tend to be solid at room temperature and are the most likely to increase cholesterol. I use these sparingly, when a particular flavor matters. Coconut oil is a good example. Mono- and poly-unsaturated fats are very good for cardiovascular health, and I don't worry about limiting these too much. A good example is olive oil.*

So here is what is in my pantry:

OLIVE OIL: *a staple for its great flavor and health benefits. There are varieties infused with flavors like lemon, lime, blood orange, or herbs like rosemary. The downside is a relatively low smoke point.*

AVOCADO OIL: *a new favorite of mine. It has a very neutral flavor, lots of heart-healthy fats, and a very high smoke point. Great for pan-searing and also for baking.*

SESAME OIL: *a richly flavored oil with a medium-high smoke point. It's great in small amounts for flavor, added to a high-temperature cooking oil for a stir-fry, or in an Asian dressing.*

COCONUT OIL: *also richly flavored and with a high smoke point. It's lovely in Thai dishes but high in saturated fat, so not an everyday oil.*

Experiment and remember that good oils are worth the investment.

GRILLED STEAK WITH CHIMICHURRI

SERVES 4

This is a meal with big flavors—a seasoned, grilled steak topped with a vibrant, tangy herb sauce that is a wonderful addition to any cooking repertoire.

I was teaching this recipe to a group of physicians when one confessed her chimichurri-phobia. Her food processor had once exploded the sauce all over her clothes, and she had avoided it ever since! Her team took the "rustic" route—no food processor necessary. She was thrilled to find a "safe" way to make this great accompaniment.

FOR THE CHIMICHURRI

1 cup cilantro leaves, about ½ bunch

1 cup parsley leaves, about ½ bunch

2 tablespoons fresh oregano leaves (or 1 tablespoon dried oregano)

3 tablespoons red wine vinegar

2 tablespoons minced shallots, about ½ shallot

¼ teaspoon salt

1 pinch red chili flakes

½ cup olive oil

2 to 3 tablespoons vegetable oil

2 (10-ounce) sirloin steaks

1 teaspoon kosher salt

1 teaspoon ground black pepper

1. To make a smooth version of chimichurri, pulse cilantro, parsley, oregano, vinegar, shallots, salt, and chili flakes in a food processor. Add oil slowly, with the processor running, until the sauce comes together and is the texture you want.

2. For a more rustic version, finely chop cilantro, parsley, and oregano. Add to a bowl and stir in vinegar, minced shallots, salt, chili flakes, and oil. Let sit for a few minutes while you cook the steaks. Give the sauce a good stir before serving.

3. Oil grill pan with vegetable oil and preheat on high. Season steaks generously on both sides with salt and pepper.

4. Place steaks on the hot grill pan and cook 5 to 6 minutes. Flip and cook on the other side, another 5 to 6 minutes, until desired doneness.

5. Allow to rest for 5 minutes. Slice on the bias, against the grain.

6. Top with 1 to 2 tablespoons chimichurri per serving.

ROASTED LEMON CHICKEN WITH CRISPY SAGE LEAVES

SERVES 6

I love roasting chickens. They make the house smell amazing and always can be counted on for a great family meal. This recipe came from rummaging around my kitchen: I had a sage plant, a bunch of thyme, and two lemons. The result was delicious!

1. Preheat oven to 450°F.

2. Rinse chicken with cold water and pat dry with paper towels. Season the inside of the cavity generously with salt and pepper. Stuff cavity with onion, lemon, half of the sage, and all of the thyme.

3. Tie chicken's legs together with twine so they are snug against the bird. Place bird breast-side up on a rack in a roasting pan.

4. With your fingers, gently loosen skin from the breast meat. Slide in lemon rounds, 2 or 3 per side. Then season outside of chicken with salt and pepper, and rub with olive oil.

5. Place in oven and cook until skin turns a beautiful golden brown, about 20 minutes. Turn oven down to 350°F.

6. Cook until a thermometer placed in the deep part of the thigh registers 160°F, 45 to 60 more minutes. Take out chicken and allow to rest at least 5 minutes.

7. Melt butter in a shallow pan. When it bubbles, add remaining sage leaves and cook until crispy, about 2 minutes. Remove from heat.

8. Slice chicken, and garnish with crispy sage leaves. If you happen to get a drizzle of the brown butter on the chicken as well, all the better!

1 roasting chicken, preferably organic, 4 to 5 pounds

1 teaspoon kosher salt, plus more to taste

1 teaspoon ground pepper, plus more to taste

1 yellow onion, quartered

2 lemons, one sliced into ¼-inch rounds, one quartered

1 bunch sage, set aside about 10 leaves for garnish

1 bunch thyme

2 tablespoons olive oil

2 tablespoons butter

SAUTÉED SHRIMP & GARLIC

SERVES 4-6

This is one of the recipes we teach to the medical students in our "The Doctor Is In . . . The Kitchen" class at Stanford. The students are amazed at how quick and flavorful this dish is, and I am always thrilled when they make this on their own and impress their friends and roommates.

These shrimp are great wrapped in lettuce and topped with salsa, or served with a good whole-grain pasta.

2 teaspoons olive oil (or grapeseed, canola, or avocado oil)

4 cloves garlic, pressed or minced

Pinch red chili flakes (optional)

1 pound large or jumbo shrimp, peeled and deveined

Kosher salt, to taste

Freshly ground black pepper, to taste

1. Heat oil in a sauté pan until shimmering. Add garlic and chili flakes, if using, and stir until fragrant, 30 seconds. Do not allow garlic to brown, or it can become bitter.

2. Add shrimp and cook, stirring occasionally, until pink on the outside and no longer translucent in the middle, 3 to 5 minutes. Season with salt and pepper.

CHEF'S TIP
FRESH OR FROZEN?

It is true that fresh is often best. Since I grew up near the coast in New England, we loved having freshly caught seafood (especially lobster right off the boat).

But now that I am a working parent, I can't always get to the store the same day I want to make seafood. I find that frozen shrimp are a very good option. They are typically frozen at sea and can maintain their fresh flavor. I keep some on hand so I can make this quick dish without a trip to the store.

TOFU LETTUCE WRAPS

SERVES 4

This recipe was born when we had been gone for a long weekend and came home to a near-empty fridge. All I could find was some lettuce, a box of tofu, a bottle of hoisin sauce, a red cabbage, and two lonely carrots. What seemed grim has turned into a new family favorite!

This recipe is also great with ground turkey, chicken, or pork. Feel free to pile on more vegetables!

1. Heat oil in a medium sauté pan until shimmering. Crumble in pressed tofu, taking care not to splatter oil.

2. Stir frequently as tofu cooks. Add hoisin sauce until tofu is all covered. Add lime juice and season with salt and pepper. When tofu is lightly browned and sauce is heated through, remove from pan and set aside.

3. In the same pan, add carrots and red cabbage, and gently stir until slightly soft and heated through, about 2 minutes. Add to tofu mixture and combine. If you prefer your vegetables crunchy, skip cooking the carrots and cabbage and add the raw carrot and cabbage to the tofu mixture.

4. Place 3 lettuce leaves on each plate. Top with 2 to 3 tablespoons of tofu mixture. Top with scallions, chopped cilantro, and Sriracha, and serve.

NOTE: To press tofu, line a plate with paper towels. Place the tofu block on the paper towels and put another layer of paper towels on top. Put a plate on top of the paper towels and add a bit of weight, like a can of beans. Allow tofu to drain for 20 to 30 minutes. Remove wet towels and pat tofu dry before crumbling and cooking.

1 tablespoon avocado oil (or substitute canola, grapeseed, or safflower oil)

1 (14-ounce) box extra-firm tofu, drained, excess water pressed out (see note)

2 tablespoons hoisin sauce

1 tablespoon lime juice

Kosher salt, to taste

Freshly ground pepper, to taste

2 carrots, grated or cut in a fine julienne

¼ head red cabbage, grated or thinly sliced

1 head Bibb lettuce (also called Boston or butter lettuce), leaves carefully removed, washed, and dried (12 leaves)

FOR GARNISH

3 scallions, sliced

½ bunch chopped cilantro

3 tablespoons Sriracha

ROASTED SALMON WITH FARRO

SERVES 4

This recipe has all of my favorite elements of healthy, delicious eating. The roasted salmon pairs well with farro—my favorite whole grain. The lemony parsley pesto brings everything together. It is a simple, elegant dish that is easy enough for weeknight eating and also a lovely meal to serve to guests.

1. Preheat oven to 375°F. Line a baking sheet with parchment paper.

2. Bring 6 cups of salted water to a boil. Add farro and cook until tender but still with a bite to the grain, 15 to 18 minutes. Drain and stir in 1 tablespoon olive oil to prevent sticking.

3. While farro is cooking, brush salmon with 1 tablespoon olive oil, and season with salt and pepper. Place on a baking sheet.

4. Roast salmon in the oven 12-18 minutes, until desired doneness.

5. While salmon is cooking, toast pine nuts in a dry skillet until brown and fragrant. Remove quickly from heat and transfer to a plate lined with a paper towel to cool.

2 cups farro

2 tablespoons plus ⅓ cup olive oil, divided

4 (4-ounce) salmon fillets

¼ teaspoon Kosher salt, plus more to taste

Ground black pepper

¼ cup pine nuts

2 bunches parsley (about 3 cups loosely packed leaves)

Juice and zest of 2 lemons

Lemon wedges, for serving

6. In a food processor, pulse together parsley, pine nuts, lemon juice and zest, ¼ teaspoon salt, and ⅓ cup olive oil.

7. Taste and adjust seasonings.

8. Toss parsley pesto with farro.

9. Plate a serving of farro and top with a salmon fillet.

10. Serve with lemon wedges

CHEF'S TIP
TOASTING NUTS

Toasting nuts is a simple technique that does wonders to bring out their flavor. You can toast nuts in the oven or in a skillet on the stovetop. I always use the stovetop method. I can keep a close eye on them that way.

STOVETOP METHOD:
Heat a skillet over medium heat. Add nuts to dry pan. Stir with a spatula or wooden spoon as the nuts cook. You should see parts of the nuts browning as you stir them. Watch them carefully, as they can burn easily.

Once they are browned and fragrant, remove immediately from heat and transfer to a plate to cool.

OVEN METHOD:
Preheat oven to 350°F. Place nuts on a baking sheet lined with parchment paper. Roast until nuts are brown and fragrant, about 5 minutes.

Transfer parchment paper with nuts from the hot baking sheet onto the counter to cool. Roasted nuts can be stored in an airtight container for up to 2 weeks.

VEGGIE QUINOA BURGERS

MAKES 6-8 PATTIES

I don't subscribe to the concept of sneaking vegetables into dishes and not telling your kids. I feel they should know what they are eating and decide if they like it or not. Except when it comes to mushrooms. My son swears he doesn't like them, but he loves these mushroom-filled burgers. So healthy and delicious!

1. If you're baking the patties, preheat oven to 425°F. Line a baking sheet with parchment paper and set aside. If you prefer to pan-fry them, see below.

2. Wipe mushrooms clean with a damp cloth. Place mushrooms, onion, and garlic in a food processor, and pulse until crumbly.

3. Heat a sauté pan over medium-high heat. Add oil, mushroom mixture, Worcestershire sauce, rosemary, and thyme. Cook, stirring occasionally, until mixture is slightly browned, 4 to 5 minutes. Remove from heat and let cool.

4. Once it's cooled, place mushroom mixture in a large bowl. Add eggs, cooked quinoa, and breadcrumbs. Using your hands, gently mix everything together and form into 6 to 8 patties. Place burgers in the refrigerator, allowing them to firm up, about 15 minutes.

5. At this point, patties can be individually wrapped and frozen for future use. Thaw before cooking.

6. Place patties on prepared baking sheet and bake 30 to 35 minutes.

You can also cook the patties on top of the stove: Heat a large pan over medium-high heat. Add oil and burgers. Cook for 4 to 5 minutes on each side, until slightly browned and crisp.

NOTE: For 1¼ cups of cooked quinoa, combine ½ cup dried quinoa with 1 cup water in a small pot. Bring to a boil. Reduce heat, cover with lid and simmer, about 15 minutes.

2 (8-ounce) packages cremini mushrooms

1 small yellow onion, roughly chopped

2 cloves garlic, roughly chopped

1 tablespoon olive oil, plus more if pan-frying the burgers

2 teaspoons Worcestershire sauce

½ teaspoon fresh rosemary

1 teaspoon fresh thyme

2 large eggs, beaten

1¼ cups cooked quinoa (see note)

1 cup whole-wheat breadcrumbs

WEEKNIGHT CHICKPEA CURRY

SERVES 4

We all love Indian food, but it can be time-consuming to make well. I wanted a way to make these flavors accessible any night of the week. A jar of curry paste does the trick! I also always try to have coconut milk and chickpeas in the pantry so I can pull this dish together anytime.

1. Heat a sauté pan over medium heat; add oil. When oil is hot, add shallot and pepper and sauté until soft, 4 to 5 minutes. Add garlic and ginger and cook a minute more. Add curry paste, stir, and cook 2 to 3 minutes more until well combined and fragrant.

2. Add coconut milk; stir to combine.

3. Add chickpeas and simmer until heated through, 15 minutes or so.

4. Serve curry over brown rice, and garnish with cilantro.

1 tablespoon coconut oil

1 shallot, minced

1 red or yellow pepper, diced

2 cloves garlic, minced

1 (1-inch) piece fresh ginger, peeled and minced (about 1 tablespoon)

1 (4-ounce) jar red curry paste

2 (13.5-ounce) cans coconut milk

1 (15.5-ounce) can chickpeas, rinsed and drained (or 2 cups cooked chickpeas)

2 cups cooked brown rice

2 tablespoons chopped cilantro, for garnish

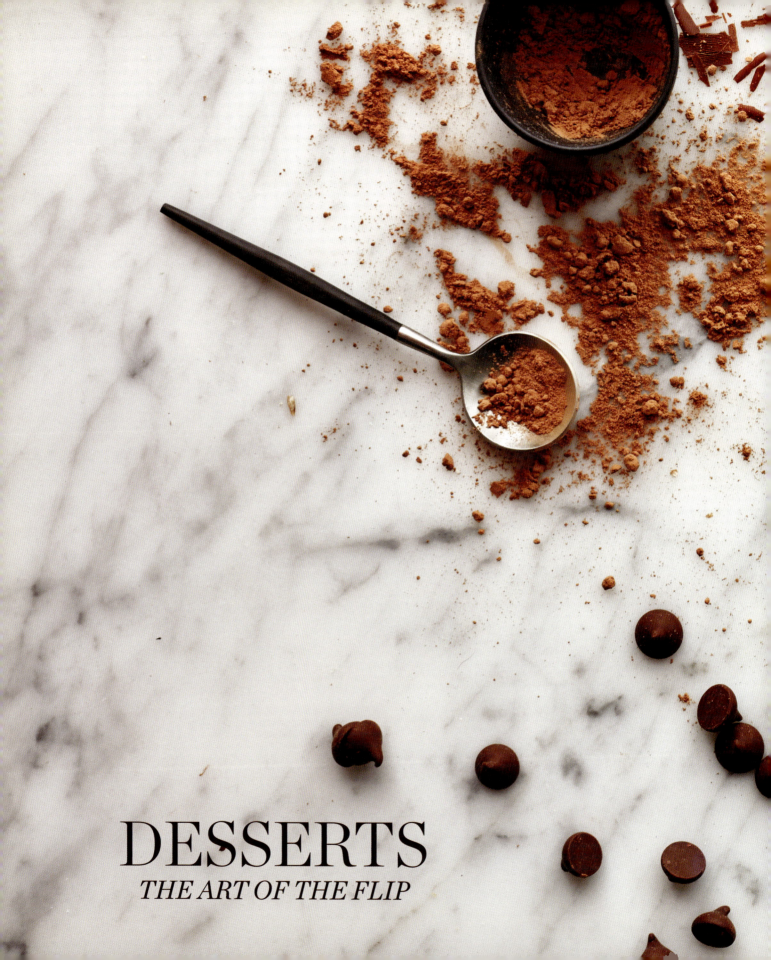

DESSERTS
THE ART OF THE FLIP

On a beautiful spring day in Napa Valley in 2008, I took a workshop at the Culinary Institute of America that would change my life forever.

The workshop was called "The Dessert Flip." The idea behind it was very simple: flip the components of dessert to make it, well, less hazardous to your health. Instead of garnishing a rich dessert with a sliver of fruit—think New York cheesecake with a strawberry slice on top—base a dessert on a sweet and delicious fruit component and garnish it with something rich and creamy. Brilliant!

The desserts we learned to make varied in complexity. There was the simple art of dipping fruit in melted dark chocolate. We took succulent strawberries, cantaloupe, and kiwi, and made them divine with a touch of dark chocolate and crispy nuts. We topped a light pastry crust with mounds of tart blueberries. We grilled pineapple and served slices alongside a silky almond-milk sorbet. Simple, yet extraordinary.

This blew my mind for a couple of reasons.

First, it struck me that there was this incredible, vast world of culinary arts that I wanted to be a part of. The sensory experience of learning to cook from talented, enthusiastic chefs was so much richer than reading cooking magazines. That week I decided I would somehow, some way, go to culinary school.

I also learned that you don't have to leave dessert behind in the pursuit of good health. Sweets and treats can fit into a healthy eating pattern. It just takes a little bit of thought, a tiny bit of skill, and the mindful intent to eat dessert *well*.

These recipes honor that concept and are meant to help you learn a few ways to savor sweet things in a new, better way.

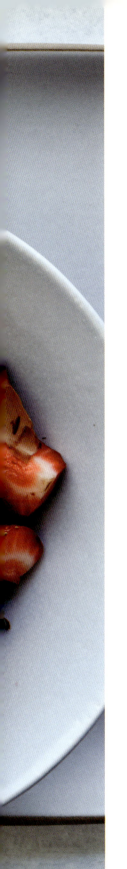

STRAWBERRY SUNDAE

SERVES 4

When my kids were little, I could get away with calling this a sundae. Now they are quick to point out the missing hot fudge and ice cream. But they still happily eat it. There is nothing like succulent, in-season strawberries and beautiful whipped cream.

1. Wash berries and remove stems. Slice them into quarters. Divide evenly among 4 bowls.

2. Place cream, sugar, and vanilla extract in the metal bowl of a stand mixer. Whip on high speed until soft peaks form. Taste and add more sugar if you like.

3. Top berries with whipped cream and chocolate curls.

NOTE: Chocolate curls are easy to make and look so elegant. Just take a bar of dark chocolate and draw a vegetable peeler along the edge to create curls.

1 pound strawberries, freshly picked if possible

½ pint (1 cup) whipping cream

1 to 2 heaping teaspoons powdered sugar

1 teaspoon vanilla extract

Dark chocolate curls, for garnish

ALL ABOUT SWEETENERS

Last week I bumped into a good friend by the honey booth at the farmers market. She was a bit surprised to see me enthusiastically sampling the various kinds of honey. Don't I worry about sugar?

I worry about some kinds of sugar. I worry about sports drinks, sodas, Frappuccinos, chai lattes, and smoothies that have three days' worth of sugar in them. I worry about all the added sugars in cereals, granola bars, protein smoothies, and other products that pretend to be healthy. I worry a lot about those kinds of sugar.

Sugar at home is different. I am not afraid to add a teaspoon or two to my coffee or my steel-cut oats. I love plain yogurt but find it a bit too tangy; a drizzle of maple syrup makes it perfect for me. I also don't worry about the sugars in whole fruit or in dairy products. These are not added sugars, which is what we all need to be careful about.

As we navigate our food world, it is helpful to remember that one teaspoon of sugar is 4 grams. Sugar, brown sugar, honey, and maple syrup all have about the same sugar content. They differ in flavor, however, and enhance dishes in different ways. I use them all for various dishes, and I am thoughtful about the amount of sugar I use.

Food companies think differently. Sugar helps food sell. For them, more is better! It amazes me how much sugar is in the foods all around us, particularly in foods marketed to children. It takes a lot of work to stay within the recommended limit for added sugar: 36 grams for men (9 teaspoons), 28 grams for women (7 teaspoons), and no more than 25 grams (about 6 teaspoons) for children.

The major contributors to added sugar in our diets are packaged foods and drinks. Many breakfast cereals, for example, have 12 to 15 grams of sugar per serving, around 3 to 4 teaspoons. Flavored yogurts can have 16 to 20 grams of added sugar per container—about 4 to 5 teaspoons.

A cup of orange juice (even fresh squeezed) has 36 grams, which is not far behind the 39 grams found in a can of regular Coke (almost 10 teaspoons). Popular drinks like chocolate milk and lemonade can have up to 64 grams of sugar in a 20-ounce bottle—16 teaspoons! Some of the sweetest drinks are marketed as healthy fruit blends; a medium strawberry smoothie in a juice shop has a dizzying 66 grams of sugar! And a wildly popular afternoon coffee drink, the Venti Iced Mocha Frappuccino, gives you 81 grams of the sweet stuff. Yikes! No wonder it is hard to stay within the recommended limit.

Adding sugar on your own enables you to control the amount and get the flavor you want. A teaspoon of maple syrup in plain yogurt, for example, will give you much less sugar than that in a presweetened variety. And in baking, you typically can cut the sugar quantity by half without compromising flavor. Don't forget to take advantage of the natural sweetness that comes in fruit. You will get added benefits without piling on the sugar.

Remember what your grandmother said: You can be sweet and smart at the same time!

APPLE CRISP

SERVES 6-8

I grew up in New England, which means that every fall was filled with apples. We never missed a seasonal trip to the apple orchard, where we would overfill our bags with the crispest, juiciest apples around. My all-time favorite is still apple crisp with a scoop of French vanilla ice cream.

1. Preheat oven to 375°F. Lightly butter an 8x8-inch square baking dish or individual baking dishes.

2. Peel and cut apples into ¼- to ½-inch slices. Try to slice them evenly for even cooking.

3. Toss apples with lemon juice, vanilla, sugar, cinnamon, and nutmeg and allspice, if using. Taste and adjust seasonings. Arrange in the baking dish.

4. Mix together almond meal, all-purpose flour, oats, butter, sugar, salt, and pecans, if using, in a bowl, using a pastry cutter or two knives to cut in the butter.

5. Spread topping over apple mixture. Bake until filling is bubbly and topping is golden brown, 30 to 40 minutes.

6. Serve with a dollop of vanilla whipped cream or a scoop of vanilla ice cream.

CHEF'S TIP

FRUIT FORWARD

A fruit crisp isn't limited to apples. Use this recipe as a springboard to try different fruit-and-spice combinations.

For the apples, cinnamon, allspice, and nutmeg, substitute:

- 5 ripe pears, diced, and 2 teaspoons ground ginger
- 4 cups sliced peaches, 1 cup blueberries, and 1 teaspoon each cinnamon and ground ginger
- 3 cups blackberries, 1 cup pitted cherries, and 1 teaspoon vanilla extract

Feel free to use your imagination!

FOR THE FILLING

3 green apples

2 red apples (such as Fuji or Honeycrisp)

Juice of 1 lemon

1 teaspoon vanilla extract

2 tablespoons sugar

2 teaspoons cinnamon

1 teaspoon nutmeg (optional)

1 teaspoon allspice (optional)

FOR THE TOPPING

½ cup almond meal

½ cup all-purpose flour

1 cup rolled oats

6 ounces cold butter, diced, plus more for pan

¼ cup brown sugar

¼ teaspoon kosher salt

¼ cup chopped pecans (optional)

Vanilla whipped cream, for serving

Vanilla ice cream, for serving

CHERRY CLAFOUTI

SERVES 8-10

My first true experience of local, seasonal eating occurred in France during a semester of college. My French mother, Monique, toted me around to the butcher, the cheesemaker, and—my favorite—the farmers market. She handed things off to me to fill our bags as she chatted and haggled with shopkeepers.

Cherries were in season that month, and Monique made a dish that seemed to suspend them in crepe batter. She served it for breakfast, wrapped a slice for my lunch, and presented it to me as an afternoon snack.

Many years later, at a market bursting with cherries, I thought of Monique and the wonderful food she made for me. Here is my best rendition of her clafouti.

3 cups sliced cherries, pits removed (about 2 pounds)
½ cup all-purpose flour
¼ cup almond meal
½ cup sugar
3 extra-large eggs
1 teaspoon vanilla extract
1 cup 2 percent milk
Pinch kosher salt
Powdered sugar, for dusting.

1. Preheat oven to 375°F. Butter a square 8x8-inch baking dish.

2. Arrange cherries in the baking dish.

3. Combine flour, almond meal, and sugar in a mixing bowl.

4. In a blender or high-speed mixer, beat eggs until pale and foamy, about 1 minute. Add vanilla. Slowly add in half the flour mixture, then half the milk, and blend on low speed. Add remaining flour mixture, milk, and salt. Blend only until combined, just a few seconds.

5. Pour mixture over cherries. Bake for 30 to 35 minutes, until a cake tester inserted into the middle comes out clean. The filling should be puffed and browned.

6. Top with powdered sugar. Serve warm or at room temperature.

LEMON POUND CAKE WITH BLUEBERRY COMPOTE

SERVES 12

I adore traditional pound cake but wanted to give it a bit of an upgrade. This recipe pairs two of my favorites—lemons and blueberries. My partner in doctor-chef crime, Michelle, helped me figure out how to honor the light, zesty flavor of lemon while making this dessert a little more heart-friendly.

1. Preheat oven to 350°F. Grease and flour a round 9-inch baking pan.

2. In a large mixing bowl, whisk together all-purpose and whole-wheat flours, baking powder, and salt. Set aside.

3. In a separate bowl, whisk together eggs, olive oil, sugar, lemon zest and juice, and vanilla. Mix thoroughly. Gently stir in yogurt until combined.

4. Working in batches, gently stir together the wet and dry ingredients until combined.

5. Pour batter into prepared pan and bake until a toothpick inserted into the center comes out clean, 33 to 35 minutes.

6. While cake is baking, heat water over medium heat until simmering. Add blueberries and sugar, stir, and bring to a boil. Reduce heat and simmer, stirring frequently, until some berries have burst and sauce is thick, about 10 minutes.

7. Serve a slice of cake with 2 tablespoons blueberry sauce. Dust with confectioners' sugar.

1 cup all-purpose flour
½ cup whole-wheat pastry flour
2 teaspoons baking powder
½ teaspoon salt
3 eggs
½ cup olive oil
¾ cup sugar
Zest and juice of 2 lemons
1 teaspoon vanilla extract
¾ cup plain whole-milk yogurt

FOR THE COMPOTE

½ cup water
2 cups blueberries
2 teaspoons sugar

Confectioners' sugar, for dusting

CHOCOLATE SILK PIE

SERVES 10-12

This vegan dessert is unbelievably smooth, rich, and delicious. It gets two thumbs up from all my die-hard chocolate lovers.

1. Preheat oven to 350°F. Grease a 9-inch pie plate and set aside.

2. In a food processor, pulse graham crackers until crumbly. Pour into a mixing bowl and add melted butter. Stir until mixture comes together. It should feel like a crumbly dough.

3. Press mixture into pie plate and bake for 12 to 15 minutes, until set. Allow to cool completely on a wire rack.

4. While crust is baking, place water in a heavy-bottomed saucepan over medium heat. Once water starts to simmer, turn to low. Place a metal mixing bowl on top of saucepan (it shouldn't touch the water) and add chocolate. Melt slowly, stirring frequently. Take care not to get any moisture in the warm chocolate, as this can cause the chocolate to "break" or clump. When chocolate is melted, cool completely.

5. When chocolate is fully cooled, slowly stir in milk and vanilla.

6. In a food processor or high-powered blender, blend chocolate mixture, agave, tofu, salt, and espresso powder until it has a pudding-like consistency. Taste and adjust by adding more agave, salt, or espresso powder as needed.

FOR THE CRUST

1 sleeve whole-grain graham crackers (9 crackers)

⅓ cup vegan butter, melted

FOR THE FILLING

2 cups water

2 cups dark chocolate (such as Trader Joe's® 72 percent cocoa bar), chopped

½ cup nondairy milk (almond or coconut)

1 tablespoon vanilla extract

3 tablespoons agave syrup

1 (14-ounce) block silken tofu, drained and patted dry

¼ teaspoon salt

1 tablespoon espresso powder

1 to 2 tablespoons confectioners' sugar

Coconut whipped cream, for serving (see sidebar)

Chocolate curls, for garnish

7. Pour chocolate mixture into prepared pie pan and chill for 2 to 3 hours.

8. Slice pie and serve with a dollop of whipped cream.

9. Garnish with chocolate curls.

WHIP IT UP!

Coconut whipped cream is a great substitute for those who don't eat dairy but still like a light, creamy dessert topping.

Chill a 13.5-ounce can of regular coconut milk (not light) in the refrigerator overnight. Remove the coconut milk from the fridge. Without mixing, scrape out the top, thickened cream and leave the liquid behind. (Discard liquid or reserve for another use—as a smoothie ingredient, for example.)

Place cream in the bowl of a stand mixer and whip until creamy, about 1 minute. Add 2 tablespoons powdered sugar and mix until smooth, another 5 seconds.

MEXICAN WEDDING COOKIES

MAKES ABOUT 24 COOKIES

My mother-in-law makes these absolutely irresistible cookies—also known as Russian tea cakes—every Christmas. I am known to sneak through the pantry to get at these cookies before everyone else. Thankfully, there are plenty to share.

1. Beat butter and sugar together until creamy. Stir in vanilla.

2. In a separate bowl, mix together flour and salt. Stir in nuts. Slowly mix flour mixture into butter mixture. Cover and refrigerate until dough is firm, 30 minutes to 1 hour.

3. Meanwhile, preheat oven to 400°F. Line a baking sheet with parchment paper.

4. Shape dough into 1-inch balls and place on baking sheet.

5. Bake for 10 to 12 minutes.

6. While cookies are still warm, roll in confectioners' sugar. Cool. Roll in confectioners' sugar again.

7. Store at room temperature in an airtight container up to 5 days—if they aren't gone by then!

1 cup soft butter

½ cup sifted confectioners' sugar, plus more for rolling cookies

2 teaspoons vanilla extract

2¼ cups all-purpose flour

½ teaspoon salt

¾ cup finely chopped pecans

MANGO ICE CREAM
SERVES 4

I bought an ice cream maker on a whim and have been surprised and delighted by how easy and fun it is to use. Just a few simple ingredients can bring sweet, delicious magic to your table.

This recipe was born out of my family's love of mangoes. You can buy mango puree at specialty stores or make your own by blending fresh or frozen mango pieces.

Top this ice cream with dark chocolate and toasted coconut if you like, but honestly, it doesn't need it.

8 ounces mascarpone cheese
1 cup whole milk
2 teaspoons vanilla extract
½ cup superfine sugar
½ cup mango puree

1. Mix mascarpone, milk, vanilla, and sugar in a mixer until very smooth. Fold in mango puree. Taste and adjust flavorings. You can add more mango or more sugar, depending on your taste.

2. Transfer mixture to an ice cream maker and churn until frozen. Enjoy right away or transfer to a freezer container until you are ready to serve.

PEACHCICLES
SERVES 6

Summer visits to my grandmother's house in New York were livened by the sing-song bell of the Ice Cream Man. My grandmother would press coins into my hand, and I would run out for the most difficult decision of the day ... did I want a chocolate éclair bar? Bomb pop? Or my stand-by—the Creamsicle? I had that sticky orange pop in mind when I needed to make use of some frozen peaches. The result wasn't quite the same, but it was delicious!

1 (10-ounce) bag frozen peaches, thawed

2 cups plain whole-milk yogurt

½ cup freshly squeezed orange juice

2 tablespoons sugar or other sweetener, such as honey or maple syrup

Set of popsicle molds

1. Combine peaches, yogurt, orange juice, and sugar in a high-powered blender, and blend until smooth, 2 to 3 minutes. Taste and adjust with more juice or sugar as needed.

2. Pour into popsicle molds and freeze at least 4 to 6 hours.

VEGAN KEY LIME BARS

SERVES 9 TO 12

I absolutely love babies. When my friend told me she was expecting a girl, I was so excited I offered to host her baby shower. I forgot, temporarily, about her dairy allergy. Yikes! I had no idea how to host a brunch without dairy. But I took on the challenge and, I admit, it was pretty delicious! Here is one of the favorite desserts.

1. Preheat oven to 350°F.

2. Heat a dry skillet over medium heat. Add coconut flakes. Cook, stirring frequently, until coconut is fragrant and brown, 2 to 4 minutes. Remove from heat immediately. Put coconut on a plate and set aside to cool.

3. In a food processor, pulse graham crackers and almond meal together until crumbly. Pour into a mixing bowl, and add sugar and oil. Stir until the mixture comes together. It should feel like a crumbly dough.

4. Press graham cracker mixture into an 8x8-inch square pan and bake for about 15 minutes, until browned. Allow to cool on a wire rack.

5. In a high-powered blender (like a Vitamix), blend cashews, coconut cream, cornstarch, lime juice and zest, agave syrup, and salt until creamy.

6. Taste and add more lime juice if needed.

7. Pour filling over crust. Bake for 22 to 25 minutes, until filling is set. Let cool and place in the refrigerator to set and cool completely before serving. Cut into 9 to 12 bars, depending on the size you like.

8. To serve, top with toasted coconut flakes.

NOTE: For 1 cup coconut cream, chill 1 (13.5-ounce) can regular coconut milk (not light) in the refrigerator overnight. Remove can from fridge and, without mixing, scrape out the thickened cream on top and use according to recipe. Reserve liquid for another use.

½ unsweetened coconut flakes

FOR THE CRUST

9 whole graham crackers

¼ cup almond meal

2 tablespoons brown sugar

½ cup coconut oil, melted

FOR THE FILLING

1 cup coconut cream (see note)

1 cup raw cashews, soaked in 1 cup water for 1 hour and drained

2 tablespoons cornstarch

½ cup key lime juice or regular lime juice, more if desired

1 tablespoon lime zest

¼ cup agave syrup

½ teaspoon kosher salt

BROWNIE ICE CREAM SANDWICHES

MAKES 9 SANDWICHES

This is my idea of dessert perfection. If you like, you can make your brownies from scratch. It isn't hard! But once I tried this Ghirardelli brownie mix, I had no desire to go back to scratch. I am equally devoted to Häagen-Dazs: Their luscious ice cream, nestled between rich chocolate brownies, is just stunning. A warm summer night on a porch swing with a brownie sandwich... heaven!

1 box Ghirardelli Double Chocolate brownie mix

⅓ cup vegetable oil

⅓ cup water

1 egg

1 pint Häagen-Dazs® ice cream, your favorite flavor (I highly recommend mint chocolate chip, chocolate chocolate chip, or vanilla. Or all 3!)

1. Preheat oven to 350°F. Grease an 8x8-inch square baking pan, and line with parchment paper.

2. Combine brownie mix, oil, water, and egg in a large mixing bowl. Pour into pan and cook according to package directions, 30 to 35 minutes. Place pan on a wire rack to cool.

3. Using parchment, lift brownies out of pan. Transfer to cutting board and cut into 9 even squares.

4. Carefully cut each brownie in half horizontally—with a top half and a bottom half.

5. Arrange bottoms of brownies on a baking sheet lined with parchment paper.

6. Put a generous scoop of ice cream on the bottom half of the brownie, then top it with the other half. Press gently.

7. Place in freezer until ice cream sets. Serve as soon as you can.

8. If you have any sandwiches left over, you can store them in a bag in the freezer as is or individually wrapped in squares of parchment paper.

SKITTLES CAKE

SERVES 10 TO 12

I can't even pretend to like this cake. It is wildly sweet and packed with unhealthy ingredients. But when it is my Skittles-obsessed son Ben's birthday, this cake is it. He really loves it. And I love him. So on his day, I abandon every healthful impulse I have, and I make a cake that rocks his world.

1. Preheat oven to 350°F.

2. Prepare cake according to package directions. Divide using 2 round 9-inch cake pans.

3. About 10 to 15 minutes into cooking, as cake is starting to set, open the first bag of Skittles and drop the candies, one at a time, into the cake. Divide them evenly between the 2 pans. Save the second bag of Skittles for decorating.

4. When cake is done, allow to cool completely.

5. Place 1 cake layer on a cake plate, and spread 1 cup frosting on top. Place remaining cake layer on top. Spread top and sides of cake with remaining frosting. Decorate with remaining Skittles and rainbow sprinkles in whatever pattern you like.

1 box vanilla cake mix, such as Duncan Hines® French Vanilla

2 (2.17-ounce) bags Skittles® candy, divided

1 (16-ounce) can vanilla frosting, such as Duncan Hines®

2 tablespoons rainbow sprinkles (or more)

ALL ABOUT
CLEANING UP

The flip side of the fun, creative process of cooking is the boring, monotonous chore of cleaning. It is one of the main reasons we go out—not to avoid cooking but to get out of the painful time in the kitchen that follows.

One of the best investments you can make is training your kids to be productive members of your family Cleanup Crew.

This doesn't happen overnight. First, they need to be tall enough to reach the sink. Then they need to figure out how to use sponges, brushes, soap, and rags. Then they need to learn how to load the dishwasher so that things actually get clean.

It may be that engaging kids in the process requires shifting your idea of what a "clean" dish really is. Knives still coated with peanut butter will get back into the silverware drawer. Wooden spoons may be caked with onion and spinach pieces. Many dishes will need to be rewashed. And it takes hours and hours for kids to learn where everything goes so they can actually put things where you will find them again.

It is tempting to shortcut this process and just do it yourself. It is absolutely faster and gets done better.

But please. Do your children—and yourself—a favor and insist that they clean up. They don't have to love it or be eager to help. Who is? But learning to be a functioning member of the household is an essential life skill. Kids who expect to help every night turn into adults who expect to help every night. And that is the kind of person who is great to have around.

After a few years of pulling your hair out and rewashing knives, you will be rewarded with occasional moments where your kids are helpful and uncomplaining. Your job will be easier. Cooking will feel less burdensome. And, who knows, you might even get to bed at a decent hour!

INDEX

Page numbers in italics indicate photos.

A

Almond & Blueberry Waffles, *29*, 29
Amy Salad, 67
Andrew's Favorite Fajitas, *120*, 121
Angel Hair Pasta, 116
apple(s)
    Apple Cinnamon Muffins, *30*, 31
    Apple Crisp, *148*, 149
    Apples & Peanut Butter, *42*, 43
avocado(s)
    Mango-Celery Salad with Pickled Red Onion & Lime Vinaigrette, *73*, 73
    Romaine Salad with Avocado & Pomegranate Seeds, *71*, 71–72
    Summer Corn Salad, *86*, 87

B

baking sheets, using, 105
bananas
Berry-Banana Smoothie with Almond Milk, *28*, 28
Bars, Vegan Key Lime, *158*, 159
beans and legumes
    Cauliflower Tacos, *124*, 125
    Edamame Beans, *46*, 47
    Indian Lentil Soup, 100, *101*
    Kale and White Bean Stew, *102*, 103
    Lemony Lentil Hummus, 50, 51
    Minestrone, 48, *49*
    Rob's Almost-World-Famous Veggie Chili, 95, *95*
    Sweet Potato Burritos, 33
    Weeknight Chickpea Curry, *138*, 139
    Whole-Grain Quesadillas, 59, *59*
beef
    Andrew's Favorite Fajitas, *120*, 121
    Grilled Steak with Chimichurri, *128*, *129*

Benjamin Broccoli, 80, *81*
berries
    Almond & Blueberry Waffles, *29*, 29
    Berry-Banana Smoothie with Almond Milk, 28, *28*
    Lemon Pound Cake with Blueberry Compote, 151
    Strawberry Sundae, *144*, 145
Berry-Banana Smoothie with Almond Milk, 28, *28*
Bowl, Spicy Quinoa Breakfast, *36*, 37
Braised Carrots, 82, *82*
Brazilian Chicken & Rice Soup, *92*, 93–94
Breaded Chicken "Tenders," *114*, 115–116
breading technique, 116
breakfast
    about, 15
    Almond & Blueberry Waffles, *29*, 29
    Apple Cinnamon Muffins, *30*, 31
    Berry-Banana Smoothie with Almond Milk, 28, *28*
    Greek Yogurt with Cherries & Slivered Almonds, *16*, 17
    My Favorite Egg Sandwich, 34, *35*
    Our Favorite Granola, *23*–*24*, 23–25
    Pancake Perfection, 32
    Perfect Eggs, 20–22, *22*
    Spicy Quinoa Breakfast Bowl, *36*, 37
    Steel-Cut Oats with Peaches, 18, *19*
    Sweet Potato Burritos, 33
Broccoli, Benjamin, 80, *81*
Brownie Ice Cream Sandwiches, 160, *161*
Burgers, Veggie Quinoa, 137, *137*
Burritos, Sweet Potato, 33

C

cabbage
    Thai Crunch Salad, *74*, 75
cake
    Chocolate Zucchini Cake, *60*, 61
    Lemon Pound Cake with Blueberry Compote, 151
    Skittles Cake, *162*, 163
Cantaloupe & Pistachios, 56
carrots
    Braised Carrots, 82, *82*
    Carrot Ginger Muffins, 52
cauliflower
    Cauliflower Tacos, 124, *125*
    riced, 124
    Roasted Cauliflower, *96*, 97
celery
    Mango-Celery Salad with Pickled Red Onion & Lime Vinaigrette, 73, *73*
cheese
    Whole-Grain Quesadillas, 59, *59*
    Whole-Wheat Pita Chips with Goat Cheese Dip, 58
cherries
    Cherry Clafouti, 150
    Greek Yogurt with Cherries & Slivered Almonds, *16*, 17
chicken
    Brazilian Chicken & Rice Soup, *92*, 93–94
    Breaded Chicken "Tenders," *114*, 115–116
    Roasted Lemon Chicken with Crispy Sage Leaves, *130*, 131
    Thai Chicken Soup, 109
chickpeas
    Rob's Almost-World-Famous Veggie Chili, 95, *95*

168 | THE NEW FAMILY TABLE

INDEX

Weeknight Chickpea Curry, *138*, 139
Chili, Rob's Almost-World-Famous Veggie, *95*, 95
chocolate
    Chocolate Silk Pie, *152*, 153–154
    Chocolate Zucchini Cake, *60*, 61
Clafouti, Cherry, 150
cleaning up, 164
Cookies, Mexican Wedding, 155, *155*
cooking techniques
    adding flavor, 98
    breading, 116
    riced cauliflower, 124
    seeding pomegranates, 72
    steaming vegetables, 84
    stock, using, 108
    taste & adjust, 25
    toasting nuts, 136
    working with herbs, 75
corn
    Corn on the Cob, *83*, 83
    Summer Corn Salad, *86*, 87
Crisp, Apple, *148*, 149
Curry, Weeknight Chickpea, *138*, 139

D

dessert
    about "the dessert flip," 143
    Apple Crisp, *148*, 149
    Brownie Ice Cream Sandwiches, 160, *161*
    Cherry Clafouti, 150
    Chocolate Silk Pie, *152*, 153–154
    fruit crisp suggestions, 149
    Key Lime Bars, Vegan, *158*, 159
    Lemon Pound Cake with Blueberry Compote, 151
    Mango Ice Cream, 156, *156*
    Mexican Wedding Cookies, 155, *155*
    Peachcicles, 157
    Skittles Cake, *162*, 163
    Strawberry Sundae, *144*, 145
    sweeteners, 146
dinner
    about, 113
    Andrew's Favorite Fajitas, *120*, 121
    Breaded Chicken "Tenders," *114*, 115–116
    Cauliflower Tacos, 124, *125*
    Essential Marinara Sauce, *122*, 123
    Grilled Steak with Chimichurri, 128, *129*
    Roasted Lemon Chicken with Crispy Sage Leaves, *130*, 131
    Sautéed Shrimp & Garlic, 132
    Simple Salmon, 117
    Tofu Lettuce Wraps, 133, *133*
    Veggie Quinoa Burgers, 137, *137*
    Veggie Stir-Fry with Super 6 Sauce, 118, *119*
    Weeknight Chickpea Curry, *138*, 139
dips and spreads
    Goat Cheese Dip, Whole-Wheat Pita Chips with, 58
    Lemony Lentil Hummus, 50, *51*

E

Edamame Beans, *46*, 47
eggs
    My Favorite Egg Sandwich, 34, *35*
    Perfect Eggs, 20–22, *22*
    Spicy Quinoa Breakfast Bowl, *36*, 37
Essential Marinara Sauce, *122*, 123

F

Fajitas, Andrew's Favorite, *120*, 121
farro
    Farro with Skillet-Roasted Tomatoes, *78*, 79
    Roasted Salmon with Farro, *134*, 135–136
fish and seafood
    fresh vs. frozen, 132
    Roasted Salmon with Farro, *134*, 135–136
    Sautéed Shrimp & Garlic, 132
    selecting, 117
    Simple Salmon, 117
flavor, adding, 98
Freshly Popped Popcorn, 44, *45*
fruit
    Apple Crisp, *148*, 149
    Cherry Clafouti, 150
    fruit crisp suggestions, 149
    Greek Yogurt with Cherries & Slivered Almonds, *16*, 17
    Key Lime Bars, Vegan, *158*, 159
    Lemon Pound Cake with Blueberry Compote, 151
    Mango Ice Cream, 156, *156*
    Peachcicles, 157
    Steel-Cut Oats with Peaches, 18, *19*
    Strawberry Sundae, *144*, 145

G

grains
    about, *76*, 77
    Apple Crisp, *148*, 149
    Farro with Skillet-Roasted Tomatoes, *78*, 79
    Our Favorite Granola, *23–24*, 23–25

Roasted Salmon with Farro, *134*, 135–136

Spicy Quinoa Breakfast Bowl, *36*, 37

Steel-Cut Oats with Peaches, 18, *19*

Veggie Quinoa Burgers, *137*, *137*

Granola, Our Favorite, *23–24*, 23–25

Greek Salad, *68*, 69

Greek Yogurt with Cherries & Slivered Almonds, *16*, 17

Green Beans, Simple Steamed, 84, *85*

Grilled Steak with Chimichurri, 128, *129*

H

herbs

Grilled Steak with Chimichurri, 128, *129*

Roasted Lemon Chicken with Crispy Sage Leaves, *130*, 131

Thai Crunch Salad, *74*, 75

working with, 75

I

ice cream and frozen treats

Brownie Ice Cream Sandwiches, 160, *161*

Mango Ice Cream, 156, *156*

Peachcicles, 157

Indian Lentil Soup, 100, *101*

K

kale

Kale and White Bean Stew, *102*, 103

Kid-Friendly Kale Salad, 70

Spicy Quinoa Breakfast Bowl, *36*, 37

Key Lime Bars, Vegan, *158*, 159

Kid-Friendly Kale Salad, 70

L

lemon(s)

Lemon Pound Cake with Blueberry Compote, 151

Lemony Lentil Hummus, 50, *51*

Roasted Lemon Chicken with Crispy Sage Leaves, *130*, 131

M

mangoes

Mango-Celery Salad with Pickled Red Onion & Lime Vinaigrette, 73, *73*

Mango Ice Cream, 156, *156*

Porcupine Mango, 57, *57*

Marinara Sauce, Essential, *122*, 123

Meatballs, Teriyaki, 104–105, *105*

Mexican Wedding Cookies, 155, *155*

milk

Berry-Banana Smoothie with Almond Milk, 28, *28*

buttermilk substitute, 29

guidelines and descriptions, 26

Minestrone, 48, *49*

Miso Soup, 106, *107*

muffins

Apple Cinnamon, *30*, 31

Carrot Ginger, 52

mushrooms

Veggie Quinoa Burgers, *137*, *137*

My Favorite Egg Sandwich, 34, *35*

N

nuts

about, 54

Greek Yogurt with Cherries & Slivered Almonds, *16*, 17

Our Favorite Granola, *23–24*, 23–25

Pistachios & Cantaloupe, 56

toasting, 136

Trail Mix, 56

O

oats

Apple Crisp, *148*, 149

Our Favorite Granola, *23–24*, 23–25

Steel-Cut Oats with Peaches, 18, *19*

oils, selecting, 127

Our Favorite Granola, *23–24*, 23–25

P

Pancake Perfection, 32

Pasta, Angel Hair, 116

peaches

Peachcicles, 157

Steel-Cut Oats with Peaches, 18, *19*

Peanut Butter & Apples, *42*, 43

peppers

Andrew's Favorite Fajitas, *120*, 121

Perfect Eggs, 20–22, *22*

Pho, 108

Pickle Platter, 53, *53*

Pie, Chocolate Silk, *152*, 153–154

Pistachios & Cantaloupe, 56

pomegranate(s)

Romaine Salad with Avocado & Pomegranate Seeds, 71–72

seeding, 72

Popcorn, Freshly Popped, 44, *45*

Porcupine Mango, 57, *57*

Q

Quesadillas, Whole-Grain, 59, *59*

quinoa

Spicy Quinoa Breakfast Bowl, *36*, 37

Veggie Quinoa Burgers, *137*, *137*

R

rice

Brazilian Chicken & Rice Soup, *92*, 93–94

Veggie Stir-Fry with Super 6 Sauce, 118, *119*

Roasted Cauliflower, *96*, 97

Roasted Lemon Chicken with Crispy Sage Leaves, *130*, 131

Roasted Salmon with Farro, *134*, 135–136

Rob's Almost-World-Famous Veggie Chili, 95, *95*

Romaine Salad with Avocado & Pomegranate Seeds, *71*, 71–72

S

salad(s)
- Amy Salad, 67
- Greek Salad, *68*, 69
- Kid-Friendly Kale Salad, 70
- Mango-Celery Salad with Pickled Red Onion & Lime Vinaigrette, 73, *73*
- Romaine Salad with Avocado & Pomegranate Seeds, *71*, 71–72
- Summer Corn Salad, *86*, 87
- Thai Crunch Salad, *74*, 75
- Vinaigrette, 66

salmon
- Roasted Salmon with Farro, *134*, 135–136
- Simple Salmon, 117

Sandwich, My Favorite Egg, 34, 35

sauce(s)
- Chimichurri, Grilled Steak with, 128, *129*
- Essential Marinara Sauce, *122*, 123

Shrimp & Garlic, Sautéed, 132
Simple Salmon, 117
Simple Steamed Green Beans, 84, 85
Skittles Cake, *162*, 163

snacks
- about, 41
- Apples & Peanut Butter, *42*, 43
- Carrot Ginger Muffins, 52
- Chocolate Zucchini Cake, *60*, 61
- Edamame Beans, *46*, 47
- Lemony Lentil Hummus, 50, *51*
- Minestrone, 48, *49*
- Pickle Platter, 53, *53*
- Pistachios & Cantaloupe, 56
- Popcorn, Freshly Popped, 44, *45*
- Porcupine Mango, 57, *57*
- Trail Mix, 56
- Whole-Grain Quesadillas, 59, *59*
- Whole-Wheat Pita Chips with Goat Cheese Dip, 58

soup(s)
- about, 91
- Brazilian Chicken & Rice Soup, *92*, 93–94
- Indian Lentil Soup, 100, *101*
- Minestrone, 48, *49*
- Miso Soup, 106, *107*
- pantry items to keep on hand, 49
- Pho, 108
- Rob's Almost-World-Famous Veggie Chili, 95, *95*
- stock, using, 108
- Thai Chicken Soup, 109

Spicy Quinoa Breakfast Bowl, *36*, 37

spinach
- Farro with Skillet-Roasted Tomatoes, *78*, 79
- Minestrone, 48, *49*
- Miso Soup, 106, *107*

Steel-Cut Oats with Peaches, 18, *19*

stews and chili
- Kale and White Bean Stew, *102*, 103
- Rob's Almost-World-Famous Veggie Chili, 95, *95*

Strawberry Sundae, *144*, 145
Summer Corn Salad, *86*, 87
sweeteners, 146
Sweet Potato Burritos, 33

T

Tacos, Cauliflower, 124, *125*
taste & adjust cooking technique, 25
Teriyaki Meatballs, 104–105, *105*
Thai Chicken Soup, 109
Thai Crunch Salad, *74*, 75

tofu
- Miso Soup, 106, *107*
- Tofu Lettuce Wraps, 133, *133*

tomato(es)
- Essential Marinara Sauce, *122*, 123
- Farro with Skillet-Roasted Tomatoes, *78*, 79
- Summer Corn Salad, *86*, 87

Trail Mix, 56

turkey
- Teriyaki Meatballs, 104–105, *105*

V

Vegan Key Lime Bars, *158*, 159

vegetables. *See also* specific vegetables
- about, 65
- Amy Salad, 67
- Brazilian Chicken & Rice Soup, *92*, 93–94
- Greek Salad, *68*, 69
- Kid-Friendly Kale Salad, 70
- Mango-Celery Salad with Pickled Red Onion & Lime Vinaigrette, 73, *73*
- Romaine Salad with Avocado & Pomegranate Seeds, *71*, 71–72
- steaming, 84
- Summer Corn Salad, *86*, 87
- Thai Crunch Salad, *74*, 75
- Tofu Lettuce Wraps, 133, *133*
- Veggie Stir-Fry with Super 6 Sauce, 118, *119*

Veggie Quinoa Burgers, 137, *137*
Veggie Stir-Fry with Super 6 Sauce, 118, 119
Vinaigrette, 66

W

Waffles, Almond & Blueberry, 29, *29*
Weeknight Chickpea Curry, *138*, 139
Whole-Grain Quesadillas, 59, *59*
Whole-Wheat Pita Chips with Goat Cheese Dip, 58

Y

yogurt
- Greek Yogurt with Cherries & Slivered Almonds, *16*, 17

Z

zucchini
- Chocolate Zucchini Cake, *60*, 61

ACKNOWLEDGMENTS

Dartmouth Medical School taught me so much. My professors gave me an extraordinary foundation in the science of medicine, and showed me the art of compassionate care. But I didn't learn to feed myself well. Or how to create healthy and delicious meals, particularly when life gets busy. Or how to blend my passion for food with life as a doctor.

That was all inspired by many incredible people: My enduring friend and mentor, Dr. Mary McGowan, who writes books and prevents heart disease and makes incredible lentil soup. The fiery neonatologist Judy Frank, who saved babies and made fabulous chocolate tart. The dynamic chefs at the Culinary Institute of America who imparted wisdom like "Control your fire!" "Cook with flavor!" and my favorite, "Don't screw it up!" David Eisenberg, whose devotion to culinary medicine is unparalleled. Julia Child, who laughed and cooked like no one else. And my Comadre, who cooks - and lives - with her whole heart. They all have my enduring gratitude.

I am also grateful for the creative talents in my life. In particular, my photographer-turned-friend Jennifer Davick, who brought my vision to life with her constant encouragement and stunning photographs. She surrounds herself with talents like prop stylist Kelly Allen, food stylist Cynthia Groseclose, and recipe tester extraordinaire Katherine Knowlton. These vibrant, dedicated women all helped make these recipes look and taste delicious. I am also grateful for the gorgeous photographic contributions of Kerry Schutz, Kristina Todini, and Mark Leet.

While I have loved to write since I was a tempestuous teen, creating a cookbook is no small task. I thank my editor, Joan Tapper, who, despite her strict rationing of exclamation points, moved this book along with kindness, humor, and laserlike attention to detail. I truly appreciate Bob Morris, who oversaw the whole book, Lauren Eggert, who designed it beautifully, and Karen Cakebread, who copyedited the text meticulously. I could not have asked for a more stellar team!

I owe deep thanks to my supportive family. My ever-loving father bursts with pride at all of my accomplishments. My effervescent mother cheers me on at every turn. My adoring grandmother Grace treasured me deeply but flatly rejected my whining when I wanted to quit medical school. She set me right back on track, and my great colleagues and incredible patients keep me there. My physician-writer family – Pegasus One – keeps me writing about it all.

Above all, I thank my husband. He is my bedrock, my champion, the "concept to reality" of all of my dreams. He brews kick-ass coffee, does mountains of dishes, and is my true partner in this beautiful, imperfect journey of raising our boys. I am so grateful for our magnificent children, Andrew and Benjamin, who are truly the light and the joy of my universe.

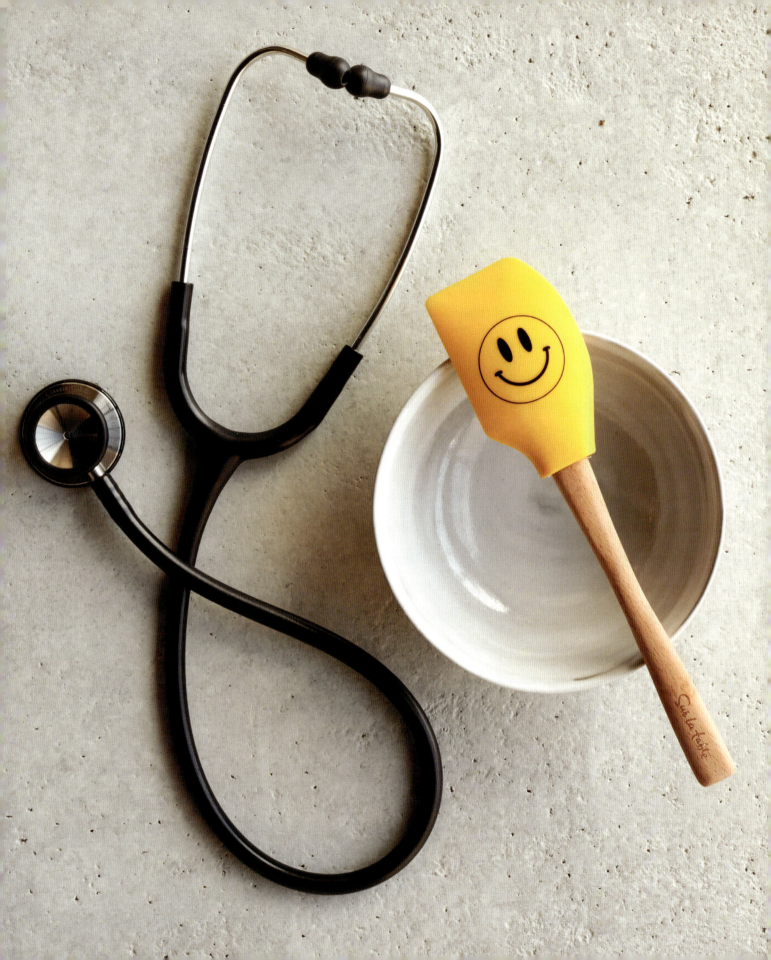